Build the Perfect
Surviva✚Kit

John D. McCann

©2005 John D. McCann
Published by

kp books
An Imprint of F+W Publications

700 East State Street • Iola, WI 54990-0001
715-445-2214 • 888-457-2873

Our toll-free number to place an order or obtain
a free catalog is (800) 258-0929.

Library of Congress Catalog Number: 2004113680

ISBN: 0-87349-967-0

Designed by Tom Nelsen & Kay Sanders
Edited by Joel Marvin

Printed in United States of America

About the Author

John D. McCann has spent years experimenting with the various components, configurations and construction techniques for making survival kits, and he has created some very unique ones. However, he continues to re-evaluate and refine his techniques in miniaturization and packaging. He enjoys teaching other people the lessons he has learned and truly believes that a survival kit can make the difference in an emergency situation.

Mr. McCann is the Chief Survival Instructor for the Wilderness Learning Center in upstate New York, offering both basic and advanced survival courses.

CONTENTS

DEDICATION & ACKNOWLEDGMENTS

First and foremost, I dedicate this book to my best friend and darling wife, Janice. During my extended trips from home for the purpose of survival training, camping and other such adventures, I am always greeted on my return with enthusiasm and excitement. She was the person who first suggested that I share my many ideas and designs for survival kits. She also endured stacks of survival components and kits laying everywhere while I designed, built and photographed them. Without her urging, tolerance and support, this book probably would never have been written.

Secondly, I would like to thank and acknowledge a good friend, Marty Simon. Although at first glance, he may appear as a crotchety old mountain man, he is truly benevolent as a friend and veraciously dedicated to the study of old, and research of new, survival techniques. He has taught me a lot about survival, and we have spent many hours discussing and sharing ideas on survival kit components and design. We have also spent innumerable days and nights in the wilderness experimenting with new ideas and concepts while sharing the best setting available: a good fire in a primitive setting.

NOTICES

It should be noted that a survival situation can be dangerous and even fatal. Although this book provides many ideas for designing and making survival kits for use in an emergency situation, a kit by itself will not assure your survival. Training in the various aspects of survival and the use of the components selected for a kit are essential. Even with that said, there are no guarantees. Neither the publisher nor the author claims that having a survival kit will ensure your survival in all situations, nor do they assume any responsibility for the use or misuse of information contained in this book.

FOREWORD

The book you hold in your hands is remarkable.

It is remarkable for at least two reasons. First, a book on building survival kits has never before been published, and secondly, the book is very good. How often do we find an original work that identifies a glaring hole in the body of knowledge and then successfully fills the hole?

John is no opportunist in this book. What I mean by that is that he hasn't just created a bunch of showy kits and offered them up as "do-this-and-you-will-survive" kits. He has actually taken hundreds of products, tested them and then worked them to their limits and beyond. He has taken the surviving products and placed them in arrangements that allow them to form mutually supporting kits that are not only effective and usable, they are dependable and reasonable to assemble. They are also fun to make.

Not happy to leave us with functional and tested assemblies, John has gone into the philosophy of kits and explained the hows and whys of each piece of gear so the readers can decide for themselves just what they want in their own personal kits. It is in the customization of survival kits that we find true utility. A custom kit will be used while a "kit in a can" might languish in a glove compartment or pack, forgotten.

I've seen literally thousands of kits over the 35 years I've been teaching survival. Most of them are in a class I'd call "keepers"; you keep them till you need them. The problem with those sorts of kits is that when and if a need arises you might not recognize it and could fail to utilize the components to your potentially everlasting grief. This is because of the very human desire to conserve resources you don't really understand. Another feature of "keepers" is that even if you wish to employ them, you might not know how the components work or how they might work synergistically. John has solved those problems. When you finish this eminently readable journey through gear and application, you will know your kit, you will carry it, and you will use it at the least provocation. That is what a real survival kit is all about.

A survival kit is the epitome of innovation, and the book you hold in your hands will start you on the path to a new sort of creative thinking. Now, take my advice, bring the book to the cashier and buy it. John will take it from there.

Ron Hood

INTRODUCTION

There have been many fine books written on how to survive but none written exclusively on the subject of survival kits. Some books touch on the subject, stating kits are necessary. Some indicate they will go into detail about kits, but they usually don't. Others explain what the author or authors are carrying for a survival kit and usually only show theirs. However, everybody is different, and his or her survival kits should be also. Except for the basics, everybody's needs vary. For this reason, I felt a book dedicated entirely to the subject of survival kits was needed. This book is my attempt to fill that void. When you complete it, you will understand the reason you need a personal survival kit, how to select the right components for YOUR needs and how to package them for YOUR purposes. When you are done, your survival kit will be YOURS, not MINE!

I've talked to many people about the subject of survival and survival kits. I am always surprised at how many people don't realize they can be thrown into a survival situation at any time. Normal everyday activities routinely place you in situations that can ultimately become emergencies. The vehicle in which you are driving could go off the road and down an embankment. You could be injured to the point where you cannot climb back up the embankment to safety. It could be days before someone finds you. The plane in which you are flying might crash-land in the mountains, and although you are only slightly injured, you must survive until you are found. A simple hike in the woods may lead to a survival situation when you become lost and must spend the night, or you fall down and break a leg. Activities such as backpacking, canoeing, snowmobiling, driving ATVs through the woods, cross-country skiing, hunting, etc. are all activities that could place you in a potential survival situation.

WHY DO YOU NEED A SURVIVAL KIT?

Survival training teaches us that your brain is your most important survival tool, and it is your experience, know-how and good judgment that get you out of most survival situations. However, when you travel, whether it is the woods, the water or just out for a ride, a survival kit is your insurance that when something goes wrong, you will have the basics to survive. A survival kit, no matter how small, helps you "stack the deck" in your favor, and in a survival situation, you need all the help you can get.

I often ask people if they ever drive their vehicle without a survival kit, and many say yes. I ask them if they have a spare tire and a jack. Most say yes. I tell them that they have the basis of a vehicle survival kit. Of course, it is a very basic kit, but a kit nonetheless. If they have a flat, they have the equipment necessary to change a tire. This is the essence of a survival kit. You not only need the essential skills, you need to have the basic equipment to help you survive in an emergency situation.

A survival kit should be carried at all times. Some items can be carried on your person. A small kit can also be carried with you in a pocket or on your belt. The combination of the total equipment and essential skills that you have on you when a survival situation occurs is all you have. A survival kit does you no good if you don't have it on you. A great example of this is the man who was driving out in the country when he saw a beautiful stream. He pulled his car over and walked over to the bank to look down. He slipped and fell to the bottom of a ravine, breaking his leg. He had a small survival kit in his car, but he lay at the bottom of the ravine overnight until a police officer, stopping to check out his car, heard him yelling. He was cold, hungry and in need of medical attention. His survival kit could have given him comfort through the night, if he only had it on him.

Having a survival kit with you is important, but it is just as important to know how to use the items in your kit! Practice with your individual survival devices prior to needing them. A survival situation is no time to learn how to use the items in your kit.

Finally, this book is about making survival kits; it is not a survival instruction manual! For this reason, you should practice starting fires, navigation, signaling, making shelters, water purification, knife and tools usage, and other skills before a survival situation occurs.

This book will teach you the fundamentals of making a survival kit that will benefit you in any survival situation. You will learn there are many sizes and types of kits. With the knowledge you obtain from this book, you will be well on your way to being a survivor. Always remember to keep your personal kit close at hand because only then can it become the perfect survival kit!

PART ONE – THE BASICS

CHAPTER 1

THE BASICS OF PERSONAL SURVIVAL KITS

There are many types of survival kits, and they can be broken down into personal kits and vehicle kits. We are going to start with the basics, the personal survival kit.

Personal survival kits are the foundation for basic survival. They are your first line of defense. If you always maintain and carry a personal survival kit with you, you will always have the basic components for survival. I don't mean to be redundant, but the important, or operational, phrase is "always carry it with you." If you don't have your survival kit with you when you need it, you're obviously already at a disadvantage. My suggestion, after reading this book, is to build a personal survival kit, knowing, experimenting and practicing with its components, and never leave home without it.

There are many types of personal survival kits available on the market today. Some of these kits are well made and provide the basics, some are sufficient, and some are lacking in serious survival components. Although many of these kits provide the basics, the quality of the components must fit the selling price of the kit. In other words, the components are not chosen on the quality of the item, but by the price of the item. The total price of items in the kit must fit within an overall selling price that allows the kit to be affordable and within your budget.

I'm not opposed to commercial survival kits, but there are three reasons I prefer self-made kits:

1. Oftentimes a commercial kit does not provide the highest quality of components. I have always felt that you should spend as much as you can afford on components for your personal survival kit. After all, you might depend on your kit for survival, and therefore, this is no place to be frugal.

2. I believe that a kit should be designed on an item-by-item basis. In this manner, you are familiar with the individual components. By packaging your own kit, you also know where each item is in an emergency. When you buy a kit that is pre-packed, you lose the flexibility of choosing a container that offers you the space for those extra items you desire. If you do purchase a pre-packaged kit, be sure you become familiar with it before you need it.

3. Lastly, as you will learn reading this book, making your own personal survival kit is easy. You can choose your own container/components and customize it for your needs.

SELECTING COMPONENTS

THE BASICS

When putting together a personal survival kit, keep in mind the basics. The basics are important because they identify specific functions that will have to be performed in order to endure a survival situation. By understanding the functions that must be performed, you gain insight into the type of items, or components, that should be in your kit in order for you to accomplish those goals. Therefore, we must discuss the functions you will most likely be required to perform in a survival situation. The items in a survival kit should allow you to perform the following functions:

+ **Build a fire using more than one technique**
+ **Signal for help using more than one technique**
+ **Gather and purify drinking water and gather food**
+ **Navigate back to civilization**
+ **Construct a shelter in various environments**
+ **Carry out basic first aid**

Personal survival kits can be broken down further into Mini and Small Kits (which can be carried on your person), Medium Kits (which can be carried in a fanny or back pack) and Large Kits (which can be carried in a vehicle, boat, plane, etc.). The size of the kit depends on what you are doing and how much you are willing to carry. Sometimes a combination of kits is desirable, such as a mini kit in your pocket, a medium kit in your pack, with a large kit in your vehicle. Even though I am an advocate of carrying items that are multi-purpose, I also believe in redundancy.

Chapter 11, "Selecting Containers for Survival Kits," will explain how to choose a container to hold your survival kit. Chapters 12 and 13 will teach you how to build personal survival kits. They will also teach you how to pack them to make them as small as possible. Chapter 14, "Making Vehicle Kits," will teach you how to make a kit specific to the type of vehicle you are using.

SELECTING COMPONENTS

Your survival kit should be made up of different components that are selected for specific purposes. These purposes should include the following:

+ **Fire and Light**
+ **Signaling**
+ **Navigation**
+ **Water & Food Collection**
+ **Shelter & Personal Protection**
+ **Medical**
+ **Knives & Tools**
+ **Multi-Purpose Items**

THE FOUR P'S

I like to use the four P's when starting a survival kit. They are:

1. **PLAN IT:** Before starting a survival kit, plan what you want it to be. Will it be a personal-carry mini kit, or a full-blown vehicle kit? Know what you want the kit to accomplish ahead of time.

2. **PICK IT:** Spend some time to determine the appropriate components that will fit the size of the kit you desire and fulfill the functions desired.

3. **PAY FOR IT:** Determine a budget for your kit. This will prevent your having one very expensive component, like a good quality knife, and the remainder of the items being of lesser caliber, not sufficient for the task required. Distribute your available funds in a manner that will allow all the components to be of near-equal quality.

4. **PACK IT:** Lastly, you must package your kit. This involves selecting the correct container, choosing the correctly sized items to fit in that container, and then packing the container for a finished kit.

When assembling your survival kit, you should choose at least one component from each heading. Some items can serve dual purpose and meet the requirements of more than one heading. An example would be snare wire (from the Water & Food Collection heading), which can be used to obtain food, repair broken items, make a fishing pole, etc. More examples of these types of items will be addressed in the Multi-Purpose Items chapter.

SEASONAL & ENVIRONMENTAL FACTORS

Keep in mind that survival kits can also be based on seasonal or environmental factors. Of course, we cannot always forecast in what environment a survival situation may occur. That is why the basics always remain the same. However, certain additional items may be chosen for the season or environment in which a person plans on being in.

Obviously, the type of shelter and clothes chosen for a summer hike will differ from those chosen for winter activities, such as skiing or snowmobiling. This would be a seasonal factor. The items chosen for a desert environment will differ from those chosen for a mountain wilderness or jungle environment. An example would be your choosing a machete as a tool for a jungle or tropical environment, whereas an ice ax and folding snow shovel would be necessary for a snow environment. A good knife and folding saw would be appropriate for a wilderness area. Keep these variables in mind when designing your personal survival kit.

Some items chosen for a survival kit in this area of the Adirondacks in New York would differ dramatically from those in a desert, tropical or snowy area.

COMPONENT SELECTION

FAST FACTS:

The Rule of Threes

3 Seconds ...One must have a positive mental attitude.

3 Minutes ...We need to breathe. Ventilate any enclosure and beware of carbon dioxide.

3 Hours ...Warmth. We must maintain heat being lost to the cold environment through conduction, radiation, evaporation, convection and respiration.

...Shelter. Get out of wind, shielded from direct contact with rain or snow.

3 Days ...Water must replace urine, sweat & respiration or the body and mind will cease to function at a surviving level.

...Rest from sleep. Without rest, the body becomes exhausted from shelter building, gathering firewood, anxiety.

3 Weeks ...Food. While the healthy body may sustain itself for up to 3 weeks, snacks and enriched liquids help maintain fuel for warmth and stamina. Food and fire are psychological boosts also.

COMPONENT SELECTION IS IMPORTANT

Before jumping right in and making a survival kit, you should learn a little about the individual components that make up a kit. If you have a better understanding of the individual components, then you are more likely to choose the correct item to fulfill a specific need. The second part of this book deals with the specific types of items that relate to various activities. This is an important section and should not be ignored. Once you understand the basics, you will be ready to get started on your own survival kit.

Many individual items are discussed and reviewed in this book. I am not a representative of any of the companies who manufacture these items, and I have not received any free samples for review. Yes, I have actually purchased each item shown (and many that are not shown) and have spent innumerable hours playing with them, experimenting with them, modifying them and testing them (some people think I have too much time on my hands).

If you're ready to build the perfect survival kit, let's get started!

PART TWO –
THE COMPONENTS

MATCHES

CHAPTER 2
FIRE & LIGHT

One of the most important activities in any survival situation is the ability to start a fire. Fire can provide us with warmth and light and a means of signaling. It can be used to purify water, cook food, make tools and dry us when wet. Morale is an important element in any survival situation, and fire also affords us a means of comfort and companionship.

This chapter will deal with those components that are useful for starting a fire and providing you with light. You should choose two or more components for your kit in order to ensure your ability to start a fire.

MATCHES

Matches are an important component for any survival kit. However, regular stick or book matches are not advisable. The matches chosen should be waterproof and windproof if possible.

The easiest way to obtain waterproof matches is to make them yourself. Book matches can be immersed in "Thompson's Water Seal" (which can be found in most hardware stores) and allowed to dry. Although I don't recommend book matches, they make a small package when size is a factor.

What I recommend are "strike-anywhere" stick matches. I melt paraffin (the kind used for canning) by placing it in a small can and then putting that can in a pot of boiling water, so the water heats the can but does not allow water to enter the can (like a double boiler). When the paraffin melts and becomes liquid, use tweezers to dip each strike-anywhere stick match into the melted paraffin, immersing them completely. I then lay them on a piece of aluminum foil until they dry, at which time they are ready to use.

Waterproof matches, although initially waterproof, will not remain so if they are subjected to an overabundance of water. They may be fine if it is raining, but they cannot sit in water for any length of time before the water eventually soaks in, usually through the ends. Therefore, a waterproof match case is always

Shown from left to right are various match cases: a 35mm film canister, a prescription bottle, a commercial military-type match holder with rubber gasket and a flint striker on bottom, and a commercial inexpensive match holder with compass, whistle and neck lanyard.

MATCHES

From left to right, "strike-anywhere" matches that have been dipped in paraffin, "Storm" matches and "Lifeboat" matches with their own waterproof vial.

recommended to store matches in a survival kit. It can be made from various containers, one of the more popular being a 35mm film canister. Most stick matches will have to be cut down a little (make sure you do this before you waterproof them), as they are usually a little too long for a 35mm film canister. There are various plastic medicine vials that are waterproof and long enough for matches available from your local pharmacist. Be sure that when you store your matches in a case to include a striker, which can be removed from a package of book matches. The strike-anywhere matches will usually light without a striker if you have a dry surface, but sometimes a dry surface is hard to find when you're soaked. A striker maintained in a waterproof case ensures you always have a dry surface to strike your matches.

There are many commercially available waterproof match holders. You can obtain these from many sporting good stores or military surplus shops. They are durable and waterproof, but make sure you get one with a screw cap and rubber gasket. Some of these cases also have a flint striker on the container, which we will discuss later in this chapter. Some also include a compass for navigation (most are not liquid filled and are inadequate) and/or a whistle for signaling (most are not very loud but a whistle nonetheless). Navigation and signaling will be covered under subsequent chapters.

FAST FACTS:

It isn't necessary for the temperatures to be at or below freezing for hypothermia to take place. Many instances of hypothermic death have taken place in temperatures over 50 degrees F. Hypothermia is heat loss at the body core, and it results from exposure to cold with the addition of other heat-loss mechanisms or nature's elements.

There are various commercially available waterproof/windproof matches and some of them are good. Two that I recommend are "Storm" matches, which are windproof and waterproof. Unfortunately, they come in a matchbox, and therefore should be repacked in a waterproof match case, as discussed above. They are available in many camp stores, such as EMS (Eastern Mountain Sports).

Another very good product is "Windproof Waterproof Survival Matches," also known as "Lifeboat Matches." They are approved by NATO, made in England and imported by Lewis International. These matches actually burn in the strongest winds and rain and come packed in a re-sealable plastic vial with a striker on the lid. My only complaint is that the striker is on the outside, which allows it to get wet. However, if it is placed on the inside of the lid, the matches should be placed in the container face down so they don't rub against the striker causing the match heads to light accidentally. You can also place a thin round piece of cardboard between the matches and the inside of the lid and striker. These matches can be obtained from various sources such as Brigade Quartermasters (www.actiongear.com) or Exploration Products (www.epcamps.com).

DISPOSABLE LIGHTERS

Another inexpensive item that is useful for starting a fire is a disposable butane lighter. They are available in many shapes and sizes and can be purchased at any convenience store. My favorite disposables are BIC lighters. They have both small- and medium-size lighters in various colors (red and yellow are good so you can see them easily) for both mini survival kits and medium-size kits. A tip on disposable lighters is they can still be used as a flint sparker (more on flint under the following heading) even when they run out of fuel.

FLINT WITH STRIKER

The old pioneers and mountain men carried flint and steel to start fires. Today, we do the same thing, but the flint and steel have changed. There are many types of flint rods available, which usually include a small piece of steel for striking the flint rod.

Without going into a lesson on fire starting, these two items are used by scraping the steel striker along the length of flint, causing numerous sparks that you direct into prepared tinder to start a fire. Any steel can be used as a striker, including a carbon-steel knife. A hardened stainless-steel knife will also work but does not provide as many sparks from the flint as when a carbon-steel knife is used.

From left to right, the small key-ring Official Scout "Hot-Spark" flint with striker, my large 4-inch flint with a cut-down file for a striker, the Strike Force Fire Starter and the Blast Match Fire Starter.

MAGNESIUM FIRE STARTERS

The Mini-Match Magnesium Firestarter (left), a custom-made medium-size magnesium fire starter (center) and the Doan Magnesium Firestarter (right).

A flint with a steel striker is a must for all survival kits. They provide innumerable uses and work even when wet and cold. They can be small, fitting on a key ring or in a mini kit, or bigger for larger kits. A nice small one is the Official Scout "Hot-Spark," which is available from many sporting good stores or from the Scouts. It costs less than two dollars, so you can also afford one for your key ring.

For my larger kit, I had a supplier cut a 1/2 x 4-inch flint rod. I use this flint rod with a cut-down file (as my striker) when I'm teaching fire starting, so I don't use, and waste, the smaller rod I carry on my key ring and in my mini kit. I save my small one for a true survival situation.

There are also some fancier packaged models that have the striker built into the case that holds the flint rod, which prevents you from losing it or having it separated from the flint rod. One of these is called the Strike Force Fire Starter, which was originally manufactured by Gerber and is now manufactured and distributed by Survival Incorporated. This unit provides a 1/2 inch thick x 1-3/4 inches long flint rod embedded in an ABS plastic case. The steel striker, which is embedded in the lid, is 1/6 inch thick x 3/8 inch wide, and although it is 2-3/8 inches long, only 9/16 inch sticks beyond the lid. Although this is more than adequate length for striking the flint, I have found that if you tug hard enough, the steel striker will pull out farther. Of course, you don't want to make it loose and take the chance of losing it. The lid is attached to the body of the unit with a lanyard so you don't lose the lid and thus the steel striker. This unit is large (5 inches long x 1-1/2 inches wide x 1/2 inch thick – weighing 3.7 ounces) and is only appropriate for a medium to large survival kit.

Another unit, also by Survival Incorporated, is called the Blast Match Fire Starter. This is another self-contained unit and is advertised as being capable of being used one-handed. The flint rod is on a spring inside the unit, and as you push on the rod, it slides past the striker causing sparks. Several of my survival buddies and I have tested this unit several times. Although it can be used one-handed, it often causes your tinder to be knocked all over on the down stroke, resulting in your having to collect and prepare your tinder again. I've also had the small striker break away from the holder, requiring the use of another striker in order to obtain sparks.

MAGNESIUM FIRE STARTERS

A magnesium fire starter is essentially flint and steel with the addition of a block of magnesium (to which the flint is glued). Shavings from magnesium burn at approx 5400 degrees (very hot) and yet the block of magnesium will not ignite by itself (unless subjected to extreme heat). To use a magnesium fire starter, you

FAST FACTS:

The four elements leading to hypothermia are: **cold, wind, wetness** and most important, **a likely victim**. It should be obvious that many of us have been exposed to cold, wind and wetness without ever having experienced hypothermia. This is because we were prepared for the conditions. A good survival kit will help prevent you from falling prey to hypothermia, commonly referred to as **"The killer of the unprepared."**

scrape off a small pile of magnesium shavings about the size of a quarter, using a knife. You then use the sparks from the flint and steel to ignite the shavings, which ignite very easily and burn extremely hot. The advantage is that magnesium burns even when wet and will help in igniting even damp tinder. I recommend carrying a magnesium fire starter as opposed to a simple flint rod with steel.

I carry a very small magnesium fire starter on my key ring. I have it made for my students and call it the Mini-Match Firestarter. It is always available to assist me in starting a fire. I also have a larger tubular magnesium fire starter that I carry in my pack. A good commercially available unit is the Magnesium FireStarting Tool manufactured by Doan Machinery & Equipment Co. It is available at many sporting goods shops and from Brigade Quartermaster & Ranger Joe's. It is provided in military survival kits and is a good unit for all but the smallest survival kits.

TINDER

The fire-making portion of all survival training teaches us that we need tinder, kindling and fuel to have a successful fire. The tinder is the first of these elements and is anything that will ignite from a spark or at a very low temperature. Of

From left to right are cotton balls soaked with petroleum jelly, WetFire Tinder and Tinder-Quick Fire Tabs. The quarter is shown for scale.

course, while there are many natural materials that can serve as tinder, they cannot always be found or are too wet. This is why it is advisable to always carry tinder in your survival kit.

One of the easiest ways to make tinder for use in a survival kit is with petroleum jelly and cotton balls. Make sure the cotton balls are 100% cotton and not the synthetic type, which do not burn as well. Soak the cotton balls with the petroleum jelly, working the petroleum into the cotton balls with your fingers, until they are saturated. Then squeeze out the cotton balls so they are not so wet and sticky. You only need a small piece of a cotton ball, which can be pulled off, to actually start a fire. You will be amazed at how flammable these cotton balls are and how easily they are lit by a spark. They can be stored in a 35mm film canister or other such container.

There is also commercially available tinder. One such example available at most camping stores is called Fire Ribbon. It is a flammable paste in a tube like toothpaste. You squirt it out of the tube onto your tinder, and it will light even when wet. It does work, but I find the tube too big for most smaller kits. Also, if it is punctured accidentally, it leaks all over your kit.

Another type of tinder that is available commercially is WetFire Tinder, which is manufactured by Survival Incorporated. It is a small dry cube (approximately 1-3/4 inches x 1 inch x 1/2 inch), individually wrapped, that will light even sitting in water. A small pile of shavings from one of these cubes is enough to get a fire started. I have found that after several years they dry out and will not light, which is a consideration for long-term storage. I called the manufacturer, and they confirmed that if the seal on the foil package breaks, they will dry out, which affects their ability to light. They were, however, willing to replace the old stuff at no cost.

Last, but not least, is a product called Tinder-Quick Fire Tabs, which is manufactured by Four-Seasons Survival. They resemble a cigarette filter, are good in all types of weather and even light when wet. You use them by pulling the tabs apart, avoiding touching or matting the inner fibers. You then ignite the fluffed fibers with a spark, and they burn for 2 to 3 minutes. I find these tabs to be very handy, especially when making mini survival kits, like the one I make in an Altoids tin in a later chapter. These tabs are dry and can be pushed down into the various nooks, crannies and open corners, which keep the mini kit from rattling. For most of my mini kits, these are my choice. For larger kits, you can't go wrong with the cotton balls and petroleum.

CANDLES

A candle is a handy item to have in a survival kit. You can light a candle first when using matches, and then use the candle (protecting it from wind) to start a fire. This will allow you to conserve your matches. A candle also can be used for light, which improves the all-important morale factor by adding comfort to a survival situation.

Candles come in all shapes and sizes, which is important when you are trying to fit a candle in a specific kit. Candles I have found especially practical for various survival kits are emergency-type candles, camping candles, tea-light candles, and the birthday-type candles that can't be blown out.

Emergency candles come in various lengths and diameters and are usually long burning. Most range in size from 3/4 inch thick and 5 to 6-1/2 inches long, to 1-1/4 inches thick and 5 inches long. You can buy them in most grocery stores. They are

At left are various emergency candles. On the right is the Nuwick44 candle closed, open with supplied wicks and matches, and open with the small aluminum "X" stand the author made so the candle can be used as a small stove for use with a metal cup or small pot. The "X" comes apart and lays flat for storage.

usually white, but some camping stores sell them in a reddish pink color and call them "Pink Lady Candles." This type of candle is best for a medium to large kit. As you will see, all components are chosen not only for their use, but also for their size.

Tea-light candles (also called tub candles) are 1-1/2 inches thick, but only 3/4 inch high. They are packaged individually in a little metal-type cup. Several of these candles can be stored in a medium-size kit. They are handy because they don't fall over and have the added advantage of the metal cup, which can be used after the candle is gone. They don't last as long as the emergency candles, but you can carry an equal amount in about the same space.

Another style of candle that fits in most mini kits is the small birthday candle that you can't blow out. This works really well when the wind is blowing. Of course, they are usually small, about 2-1/4 inches x 3/16 inch, but fit in very little space. They are only really good for fire-starting purposes, as they don't last very long. There are regular birthday candles around the same size, but they lose their advantage without the non-blow-out benefit.

Another type of candle of which I am aware, but have not tried, is a candle made from oleo stearin vegetable fat. Allegedly, they can be eaten in an emergency situation as a calorie source. Again, I haven't tested them and don't eat candles made from paraffin wax. The only source I am aware of for these candles is Lewis International, which imports them from England.

The last candle is the Nuwick44 candle, which is ideal for medium to large kits. This candle comes in a can that is 1-1/2 inches high by 3-5/8 inches in diameter. The lid is replaceable so it can be used over and over, until the candle is used up (approximately 44 hours). It is unique in that it provides three movable and re-usable wicks, which actually float on the wax. You can use one, two or all three wicks depending on if you are using it for light, heating or cooking. They also offer a folding stove for cooking, but I find it too cumbersome for survival kits. Instead, I made an "X"-shaped stand from two small pieces of aluminum that sits on the candle and allows me to cook with a cup or small pot. I also use this candle as the base for a snow-melting stove I built that will be discussed further in Chapter 5. These candles are manufactured by Nuwick International and can be obtained from various emergency suppliers and Ranger Joe's. It should be noted that they also offer a Nuwick 120-hour candle in a can, but it is obviously larger and probably only appropriate for a large survival kit.

LENSES

Keep in mind that larger candles can be cut down to accommodate a desired container. I have one in an Altoids tin that is 3/4 inch thick but only 5/8 inch high.

LENSES

A small magnifying lens is also useful for starting a fire and can be an additional item for a survival kit. Keep in mind that it should only be a backup device, as they only work if the sun is out. Although small glass lenses are available, I have found that the small Fresnel plastic magnifying lenses work well. They are extremely thin and the one I use is 2 inches x 3-1/4 inches. I also keep one in my wallet. All the above lenses can also be backups for broken glasses in an emergency situation.

FLASHLIGHTS

When it gets dark, we have a fire and candles to give us light (if we prepared). But any source of light that we can carry around with us, and is water repellant or waterproof, is obviously an advantage. This is where a flashlight comes in. While they come in a thousand shapes and sizes, we should think about some prerequisites before choosing one. First, as usual, is size. Next, we will probably want it water repellant or, if possible, completely waterproof. We want it durable and, if possible, unbreakable. This eliminates many from our choices. We then

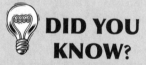 **DID YOU KNOW?**

THE SYMPTOMS AND STAGES OF HYPOTHERMIA

Air Temp / Body Temp / Symptoms

1. 47-50° F / 96-99° F = Uncontrollable shivering
2. 42-46° F / 91-95° F = Violent shivering in waves, poor coordination and stumbling
3. 37-41° F / 86-90° F = Shivering ceases, muscles are stiff, impaired thinking or judgement
4. 32-36° F / 81-85° F = Rigid muscles, slowed pulse rate & respiration, stupor, immobility
5. Below 32° F / 78-80° F = Unconsciousness, most reflexes cease, erratic heartbeat, possible death
6. Below 32° F / Below 78° F = Cardiac fibrillation, edema & hemorrhage in the lungs, white foamy discharge from the lungs, possible death
7. Certain Death!

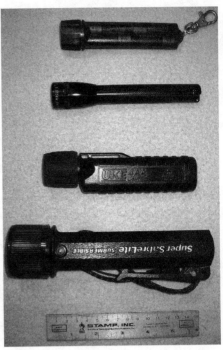

Left photo from top to bottom: Photon Micro-Light II, CMG Sonic, UKE Mini Pocket Light, CMG Infinity LED Task Light and Princeton Tec Blast. Right photo from top to bottom: Princeton Tec Attitude, Mini-Mag Light, UKE 4AA Light and Pelican Super Sabrelite.

must determine if we want an LED light (LED lights last longer than any other type light on the market), an incandescent-type light bulb, or a bright Xenon-type bulb. Battery life is longest in LED lights and discharges more quickly as we switch to incandescent and then to Xenon-type bulbs. This eliminates more choices.

Next, we must decide where we are going to package the flashlight, so we know the size appropriate for the space. Obviously, for a small place, like a mini kit, our options are again reduced. One of my favorites for mini kits is the Photon Micro-Light II. It is the smallest and most reliable light for its size of which I am aware. It can be turned on by simply squeezing it, and it has a miniature on-off switch for continuous light. It is the approximate size of a quarter (actually 1-1/2 inches long x 7/8 inch wide x 1/4 inch thick). It is an LED light powered by a replaceable lithium battery and is the brightest, for its size, I have found. I not only use them in mini kits, but also carry one on my key ring and attach them on the zippers of my jackets.

A second light of small size, which has only recently been released, is the Sonic by CMG Equipment. It is water resistant, constructed of anodized aircraft aluminum, extremely bright and powered by one AAA battery. It is 3 inches long with a 9/16-inch diameter. I started using this light because I like to use the same battery in all lights (so I only have to carry one type of spare battery) and use AAA batteries in my flashlight and headlamp. It is available from various camping stores such as Eastern Mountain Sports (EMS).

The Underwater Kinetics (UKE) 2 AAA Mini Pocket Light is another small light that has a high-intensity Xenon bulb, as opposed to an LED. Although the batteries don't last as long as with the LED lights, it is extremely bright. It has O-ring seals, is waterproof and measures only 3 inches long x 1 inch wide x 5/8 inch thick. I have been using this light for many years, and it has never failed me. I actually ran it over with my truck (by accident when it fell out of my pocket), and it still works today.

A slightly larger light is the Infinity LED Task Light manufactured by CMG Equipment. It is made from anodized aircraft aluminum and is waterproof. The burn time is 25 hours on one AA battery. It measures 3-1/4 inches long x 3/4 inch in diameter. It is an excellent light for a small survival kit.

A light that I use in all of my medium kits is the Blast Light by Princeton Tec, which is only slightly larger than the Infinity LED Task Light. It uses a high-output Xenon bulb and is one of the brightest lights of its size I have found. It is waterproof and operates on two AAA batteries (an additional reason for my choice). Batteries last about 3 hours.

Another light from Princeton Tec that I use is the Attitude. It is waterproof and has three ultra-bright LEDs that operate for 150 hours on one set of four AAA batteries.

A favorite light of many is the AA-battery Mini-Mag Light. It has been around a long time and is waterproof, reliable and well-made from aluminum. Although I never considered it very bright, it is an ideal choice for all but the smallest survival kits. You can also take off the head and use it as a base for the remainder of the flashlight, which provides a candle-type light.

Another excellent AA-battery light is the UKE 4AA Light. Only slightly larger than the Mini-Mag Light, it uses a Xenon bulb and is extremely bright. O-ring seals keep it waterproof. For its size, it is my choice for larger survival kits.

Although there are many fine choices among large flashlights, I use the Super Sabrelite by Pelican. It has 12,000 candlepower and burns from 5 to 6 hours. It uses three "C" cells and is waterproof to 500 feet. It uses a Laser Spot Xenon bulb to produce a tightly focused collimated white-light beam that really reaches out there. Although it uses the "C" batteries, it is my choice for large survival kits, with my Blast light as a backup.

Keep in mind that there are many fine flashlights out there from which to choose. Experiment and make your choice based on size, dependability, durability and brightness for the job. You can and will make trade-offs. I have picked an LED light over a Xenon bulb because of the length of burn time on batteries. The LED is not as bright but provides light for a longer length of time, and in a survival situation, I want as much burn time as possible.

HEADLAMPS

Headlamps are not a necessary item and I only use them in larger survival kits. However, they are very handy when an activity requires the use of both your hands. For smaller kits, I usually carry one of those elastic straps that have a small loop sewed onto it. I can place one of my small lights into the loop and place the elastic loop around my head. This frees up my hands.

From left to right are the Black Diamond Ion (6-volt lithium battery), Petzl Tikka (3 AAA batteries), Petzl Tikka Plus (3 AAA batteries) and the Princeton Tec Quest (2 AA batteries).

For larger kits, you may want to include a headlamp specifically designed for this purpose. Again, there are many choices. I use LED headlamps, as they burn longer than the AA-battery type.

The smallest headlamp with which I have experimented is the Ion by Black Diamond. It has two LEDs, is very small and weighs less than an ounce. It packs into very small spaces but uses a 6-volt lithium battery, which is not as readily available as AA and AAA batteries.

My choice for medium to large kits is the Petzl Tikka, which has three LEDs and operates on three AAA batteries with a burn time of 150 hours. It is small and light (2.4 oz. with batteries) and packs well. Petzl has recently offered the Tikka Plus. It has four LEDs with a switch that allows you to use it in economy mode (400 hours), optimum mode (120 hours) or maximum mode (80 hours). The fourth option allows for a blinking, intermittent mode (400 hours). It is essentially the same size as the original Tikka, except for being slightly thicker to accommodate a new bracket that allows the headlamp to be tilted down.

For a unit that uses AA batteries, there are many choices. One unit that I have used is the Princeton Tec Quest, which uses two AA batteries and weighs 4.5 oz. (twice the weight of the Petzl Tikka and over twice the size). It is waterproof and has a focused wide beam. Burn time is about 8 hours.

In order to keep it as small as possible, try not to get a unit where the battery pack is separate from the light and is connected by a cable that attaches to your belt. In my opinion, these are too big and too cumbersome. As with everything in survival, keep it simple (and as small as possible).

There are many more units that are adequate from other manufacturers. The main thing is to determine how bright you want them, how long you want them to last on batteries and, as with all items for a survival kit, how much space you want them to fill.

LIGHTSTICKS

Another helpful item for a survival kit is a Lightstick (also known as Snaplights and Cyalume Lightsticks). A Lightstick is basically a non-toxic chemical in a plastic tube. You simply flex the tube to break another internal smaller tube, allowing the chemicals to mix, which results in light.

FAST FACTS:

Frostbite looks like a serious heat burn, but it's actually body tissue that's frozen and, in severe cases, dead. Most often, frostbite affects the toes, feet, fingers, earlobes, chin and tip of the nose. These body parts are often left uncovered and can freeze quickly. Frostbite begins when these areas are exposed to temperatures that are below freezing. Frostbite can set in very slowly or very quickly. This will depend on how long the exposed skin is subjected to the cold and how cold and windy it is.

Keep in mind that these lights provide more of a bright glow than a direct light, and the light is not directional. However, being chemical lights, they do not require batteries and will last from 30 minutes to 12 hours depending on the intensity. They are windproof, waterproof and safe to use or store anywhere. They come in 4- and 6-inch lengths and can be stored in medium and large kits. I usually keep a couple of the high intensity (30-minute usage) and a couple standard intensity (8-hour usage) in my medium and large kits, as well as in my travel safety kit. These Lightsticks do have a shelf life of 4 years, so it is important to record when you put them in your kit so they can be replaced at the end of their shelf life.

FIRE BOW BEARING/SOCKET

For those who have studied survival and have already made a fire with a bow and drill, you will know the most difficult piece of the bow and drill to make in the field is the bearing or socket. This is the part you hold in your hand and in which the spindle spins. For this reason, I carry a ready-made bearing with me. I have a small one made from deer antler on my key ring, which I wear on a neck lanyard when I'm in the field. I also carry a larger one, also made from a deer antler, which hangs on my pack. Again, be prepared to survive!

Now that we have a good understanding of the fire and light components, let's move on to signaling components.

CHAPTER 3
SIGNALING

Another important activity in a survival situation is the ability to signal people who might be trying to locate you. Of course, fire can be used as a signal, but in this chapter we are going to cover signaling devices that can be carried in a survival kit, not signaling techniques (we have to leave something for survival training courses!).

SIGNAL MIRRORS

Every survival kit should have a survival mirror. It is the most underrated and valuable daytime means of signaling. There are various shapes and sizes, and, as usual, your choice will depend on the size of your kit.

A very good signal mirror that fits in all but the smallest kit is a commercial unit manufactured by Survival Incorporated (Really, I don't work for this company; they just make some good products.). Called the StarFlash Mirror, it is made of unbreakable Lexan polycarbonate and it floats. It has a small star-shaped hole in the center for sighting purposes. It has instructions printed on one side (so you don't lose them) and has a lanyard hole on one corner. The standard size is 2 inches x 3 inches x 1/4 inch and it weighs 1/2 ounce. They also offer it in 3 inches x 5 inches, but the smaller unit is more than adequate. These mirrors are available from various suppliers such as Brigade Quartermasters and Ranger Joe's.

FAST FACTS:

Pilots have reported seeing mirror flashes up to 160 kilometers away under ideal conditions.

Another mirror, which is super light, is the Featherweight Mirror manufactured by Sun Company and available at many camp stores. Larger than the StarFlash at 4-1/4 inches x 3-1/8 inches, it is only 1/32 inch thick. It is made from shatterproof Metallized

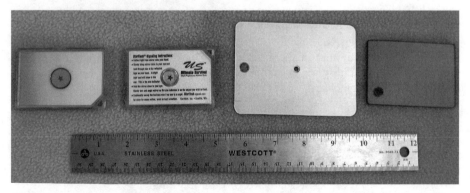

From left to right, the front side of the Survival Incorporated StarFlash Mirror, the back side of the StarFlash Mirror with instructions, Featherweight Mirror by Sun Company and red side of Safe Signal Mirror.

The auto-repair mirror material with a piece cut out and made into a signal mirror. On the far right is a CD, which can be used as a signal mirror in an emergency.

construction; it is bendable and can be slid into tight places in a kit. It also has a sighting and lanyard hole.

Although signal mirrors are normally used during the day, a new mirror introduced by MPI Outdoors called the Safe Signal was designed for both day and night use. One side has a patented mirror finish and the other side has a special red laminated surface. For daylight use, you use the mirror side. For night use, you focus the beam of light from a flashlight on the red side, which gives off a visible red beacon. It is made from polycarbonate and is shatterproof and waterproof. Measuring 2-1/4 inches x 3-1/4 inches, it weighs 3 ounces. I have experimented with this mirror and would like to see a sighting hole added, and I have not had much luck getting a "red beacon" with the night side.

If you want to make a signal mirror yourself, it is not very difficult. You can buy a kit called "Easy-Stick Replacement Mirror" in many auto parts supply stores. It is a bendable plastic material that comes in a sheet 7 inches x 10 inches x 1/16 inch thick and only costs a couple of dollars. You can cut a mirror to the size you want with scissors and still have plenty of material left over for other kits. I have made mirrors in various sizes for specific applications and punched a small sighting hole in the center using a leather punch. It has the added advantage of the self-sticking side in the event you want to stick one in the lid of a survival tin (in which case you lose the advantage of the sighting hole).

Speaking of survival tins (which we will discuss at length in a later chapter), you can polish the inside lid of a survival tin and use that as a survival mirror. As long as you have your kit, you have your mirror.

One last tip on signal mirrors: If you are stranded in a vehicle with a CD player (or if you are in a survival situation and just happen to have a portable CD player with you), a CD makes an adequate signal mirror. It is highly reflective on one side and already has a sighting hole.

WHISTLES

A whistle is a very useful device for signaling and is easy to carry. It is much easier to blow on a whistle then yell, and the sound from a whistle travels further. Also, a whistle can easily be incorporated into a survival kit, or it can be carried around your neck on a lanyard or on a key ring.

The first thing to remember about a whistle for survival is not to get a metal one. In freezing weather it can freeze to your lips. The second thing is to get a pea-less whistle. As with everything in survival, the more parts something has, the greater the chance it won't work when you need it. Also, if the pea is lost, the whistle won't work.

While there are many whistles available, we will discuss but a few that I think are most effective for survival needs. The first is the Fox 40 whistle, which has a harmonically tuned, three-chamber pea-less design. It can't be overblown and the harder you blow, the louder it gets. It will work when soaking wet and produces an omnidirectional sound. This whistle is extremely loud and is being issued to the military and Coast Guard. Available from Brigade Quartermasters, Ranger Joe's and Exploration Products, this is the whistle I carry on my key ring and pack. They are also available at many sporting good stores, as many sports referees also use these whistles.

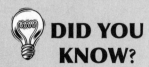 **DID YOU KNOW?**
Whistles provide an excellent way for close-range signaling. In some documented cases, they have been heard up to 1.6 kilometers away. Manufactured whistles have more range than a human whistle and are easy to carry in any kit.

A second whistle that is good for survival purposes is the Skyblazer Whistle (Skyblazer was recently purchased by Orion Safety Products, which still offers the Skyblazer products). It is a pea-less whistle designed for marine use and is waterproof. Although this whistle is not quite as loud as the Fox 40 whistle (but it is still loud), it is flatter in design and packs very nicely in small survival kits.

The next whistle is the WindStorm Safety Whistle. This, in my opinion, is the loudest whistle, but it is also the largest. It has been adopted by the U.S. military, as it can be heard above howling wind and helicopter noise. It is a waterproof pea-less design and is a good choice for larger kits. It can be purchased from the same two military suppliers as the Fox 40.

A recently introduced whistle for survival is the JetStream Whistle by Survival Incorporated. It is a loud waterproof pea-less whistle with a round flat design. It is a little larger than my first two choices.

There are several other whistles out there that were designed specifically to be survival whistles and that have various added features. One that is a reasonable whistle is the Four Function Whistle offered by Coghlan's. In addition to being a whistle, it has a thermometer, compass and small magnifier.

From left to right, the Fox 40 whistle, Skyblazer whistle, WindStorm whistle, JetStream whistle and Coghlan's multi-use whistle.

SMOKE SIGNALS AND FLARES

QUICK TIP:

If you have enough time to build a fire, try to create a color of smoke that contrasts with the background; dark smoke against a light background and vice versa. If you practically smother a large fire with green leaves, moss, or a little water, the fire will produce a heavy white smoke. If you add rubber or oil-soaked rags to a fire, you will get a thick black smoke.

It is not very loud and appears breakable. Available at many camp stores, it is in the same class as the whistle on the match case shown in the previous chapter. These whistles will do in a pinch, but I would recommend getting a higher-quality pea-less whistle that provides the volume of sound required for a survival situation.

SMOKE SIGNALS

Various companies manufacture smoke signals designed for survival use. They are small devices that give off smoke (usually orange) and are usually waterproof. They burn from 45 seconds to a minute and are an option for a survival kit if you don't have time to build a fire or are on the water. They are available from Exploration Products, but shipping them requires a Haz-mat charge.

FLARES

Survival flares are another useful item for a survival kit, especially if you are on water. They are used for aerial signaling so search aircraft can locate your position. One that I have found very reliable is the Skyblazer XLT Flare. Self-contained, waterproof and floatable, it is compact (4-7/8 inches long x 15/16 inches in diameter) and U.S. Coast Guard approved. This disposable flare can reach an altitude of 450 feet, has an average of 12,000 candlepower, and burns for 6.5 seconds. They come in a package of three and are available from Orion Safety Products.

Skyblazer XLT Flares with the one on the right open in the firing position.

Shown here from left to right are the Emergency Strobe, Firefly Plus and The Guardian.

DYE MARKERS

Another small device that can be carried in a survival kit, especially if you are on water or in snow country, is a Dye Marker. They are small (2 oz.) and packed in a waterproof container. They can be deposited on water or snow, are visible from aircraft during the day, and are environmentally safe. Orion Safety Products offers a package of two that contain a green dye that covers up to 50 square feet.

EMERGENCY STROBES

A signaling device that should be in all survival kits for water-borne operations or activities (especially for large bodies of water) is an emergency locator strobe. Also used for marking a campsite or a disabled vehicle, they come in various shapes and sizes and should be U.S. Coast Guard (USCG) approved.

A good unit for any medium to large survival kit is the Emergency Strobe, sold many places as the "Pocket Strobe." It is a small, lightweight, battery-powered strobe light that creates a beacon visible up to 3 miles. It is waterproof and flashes 50 to 60 times per minute for up to 16 hours. It uses a Xenon strobe module that produces a 300,000-candlepower light and operates on one D-cell battery. Red in color, it also has a safety-pin-type holder (actually a stainless-steel locking pin) so you can wear it on a PFD (personal flotation device) in the event of a "man overboard" situation at night. Available from Brigade Quartermasters, Exploration Products and many marine shops, this strobe is 4-1/2 inches high, weighs 8 ounces and is U.S. Coast Guard approved.

A combination emergency locator strobe and flashlight, the Firefly Plus by ACR Electronics is U.S. Coast Guard approved. This international orange unit is waterproof and operates on two AA alkaline batteries. The high-intensity strobe can be seen for over one mile and the unit floats. The strobe will operate for up to 10 hours and the flashlight for up to 2 hours. It measures 5.3 inches x 1.5 inches and will fit in most medium to large kits. Supplied with a wrist strap, it is available from the same suppliers as mentioned for the Emergency Strobe.

An extremely small unit is The Guardian by Adventure Lights. More a safety strobe than an emergency strobe, it is visible over one mile from a front view, and 1/4 mile from the side view. They are available in "steady-on" or flashing models and in various color lenses (clear, blue, green, yellow and red). They are waterproof and operate on one coin-cell lithium battery. The red and yellow models flash for an impressive 150 hours (the other models for only 50 hours). Measuring 1-5/8 inches long x 1-1/4 inches wide x 1 inch high, they are small enough to carry in a small survival kit and provide you with at least a small strobe. A small clip is included that allows you to attach the unit to almost anything. They are available from Eastern Mountain Sports.

CHAPTER 4
NAVIGATION

The ability to navigate back to civilization in a survival situation, if that is the proposed plan, is extremely important. Any good survival school will thoroughly cover navigation, to include using a map and compass, as well as ways to navigate without them. But as this is a book on survival kits, let's discuss those components you can include in a kit that will assist you in navigation.

COMPASSES

An item that should be in every survival kit, no matter how small, is a compass, which is the basic tool of navigation. They come in all shapes and sizes. The one you choose should be a liquid-filled compass (this slows the swinging of the needle, called damping, and makes the needle stop faster). With mini kits, your only choice is usually a fixed-dial compass, also called a "button" compass. It is a small liquid-filled capsule with no frills, whereby the needle swings freely, and the degree markings are on the capsule case. Size often dictates features, and with a fixed-dial or button compass, there are no features other than the ability to determine direction.

For all of my mini kits, I use a 20mm button compass that is Grade-AA (the highest grade). They are liquid filled and have a highly luminous dial. Measuring 3/4 inch in diameter x 5/16 inch thick, these are great for any tin-type survival kit.

A compass is one of those items for which I like to have a backup. Fixed-dial compasses are also available in various configurations, such as for a watchband strap, built into the top of a walking stick, or on a keychain fob. Any of these is a handy way to carry a backup for the main compass in your survival kit. Again, make sure it is a liquid-filled compass (I was given a walking stick as a gift and it had a non-liquid-filled compass on top; I am still waiting for the needle to stop swinging).

This array of "button" compasses consists of, from left to right, a 20mm Button Compass, a Suunto Clipper, a Suunto Clipper on the author's watchband, a Sun Therm-O-Compass and a Silva Key Ring Compass.

A nice wristwatch band compass made by Suunto is the Clipper, which is very accurate and has features usually only found on larger compasses. It can actually be clipped to clothes, equipment straps, etc., or even clipped inside a survival kit. It is liquid filled with a jeweled bearing and has directional points and a rotating/ratcheting dial. It even includes a wrist strap. I have had one on my watchband for at least 10 years. It is my backup that I always have on me.

Another small button compass is the Therm-O-Compass by Sun Company. It is a key fob with a thermometer and a compass module on one side and a wind-chill chart on the other. It can be carried in a mini kit or as a backup attached to the zipper pulls of jackets or a key ring.

A larger fixed-dial compass is made by Brunton and Silva and measures 1-3/4 inches diameter x 3/8 inch thick. It has directional points and makes a nice backup. Although a little large, it can also be carried in a mini kit.

There are many variations of fixed-dial or button compasses, but stick to quality units that are liquid filled, especially if it is the only compass you are carrying.

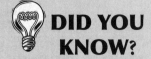 **DID YOU KNOW?**

The magnetic field of the Earth is fairly weak on the surface. After all, the planet Earth is almost 8,000 miles in diameter, so the magnetic field has to travel a long way to affect your compass. That is why a compass needs to have a lightweight magnet and frictionless bearing. Otherwise, there just isn't enough strength in the Earth's magnetic field to turn the needle.

With all other kits, from medium on up, I recommend an orienteering compass (also know as a base-plate compass). These have a transparent plastic base with a compass capsule that is independent from the base. They are designed to be used with a map to make traveling in a specific direction much easier than with a fixed-dial compass. These compasses range from basic orienteering models to advanced models with options such as sighting mirrors, adjustable declination and clinometers. Of course, if you don't have training with a compass, I recommend that you get some before a survival situation occurs!

When choosing an orienteering compass, it is a good idea to stick to the major manufacturers (some of my favorites are Brunton, Silva, Suunto and Sun). There are some cheaper options out there, but a compass is not something you want broken, or inaccurate, when you go to use it.

I also recommend a luminous dial, which is useful in the dark or in low light conditions. (Tip: If a luminous dial isn't glowing, shine a flashlight on it for a few moments and it should glow for several hours.) If you plan to use an orienteering compass in conjunction with a topographical map (more on maps later), you should get a magnetic declination adjustment feature. Although not absolutely necessary (you can always add or subtract the deviation at each reading), the stress of a survival situation could cause you to forget to make the mental calculation. If

Some orienteering compasses used by the author in survival kits. From left to right, they are a Brunton Classic, Brunton Advanced, Suunto Leader M-3 and Brunton Eclipse.

you are not familiar with declination, this may not sound important. However, if you were in the eastern- or western-most parts of the U.S., the magnetic declination can be as high as 22 degrees. If you didn't take this into consideration, you could end up more than a mile off your destination at a distance of 3 miles.

Some orienteering compasses also have a sighting mirror, which provides you with a more accurate means in which to sight your compass when navigating. Many also have a small magnifying glass in the clear plastic base. Not only can this be used to magnify the finer features of a topographical map, but it also falls into the "multi-purpose usage" category, as it can be used to see a splinter for removal, or even for fire starting.

Again, no survival kit should be without a compass. If you only have a fixed-dial compass in a mini kit, consider carrying an orienteering compass in a belt pouch or even on a lanyard around your neck.

MAPS

Before we start discussing maps, I should mention again that this chapter is not a lesson on navigation. Also, unless you maintain a survival kit for every specific area you travel, you probably won't have a map in your kit for every area in which you venture. However, if you plan a trip to a certain place, it is a good idea to include a map for that area in your kit. Finally, if you don't currently have any training with a map (or map & compass), I suggest you get some.

The most useful map for navigational purposes is a "topographical" map, which actually describes the terrain, as well as showing man-made features such as certain buildings, roads, hiking paths, etc. They show the shape of the land by using what are called contour lines. These lines show the height and steepness of the terrain (very handy when making a decision as to what direction you will travel). In the U.S., the topographical maps are compiled by the U.S. Geological Survey (USGS). There are topographical maps that cover every square inch of the U.S. (by the USGS) and actually most of the world by others. There are also topographical maps of certain areas published independently. I have several for the Adirondack, New York, area that are based on USGS and NYSDEC maps but are published by an independent company.

Keep in mind that you don't have to carry an entire map if you are only going to be traveling in a specific area of that map. I have often taken a

*Here are some of the author's topographical maps. The top right map is in a
SealLineWaterproof map holder. The map on the bottom left is a section from a
larger map color copied and coated with Thompson's Water Seal. It can be folded
and kept in a survival kit when in that area.*

section from a map (and made a color copy of it) and carried only that section.
It folds down smaller and fits better into a survival kit. Also, a map, or copy of a
section, can be waterproofed by coating it with Thompson's Water Seal. It can still
be folded and will last for a long time. If you do not waterproof your map, at least
carry it in a zip-lock bag or in a waterproof map case, available from many camp
and canoe shops.

GPS (*Global Positioning System*)

A GPS (Global Positioning System), simply described, is an electronic device
that can provide you with your current position in latitude and longitude by
communicating with at least four of 24 orbiting satellites put in space for just that
reason. Some advanced units can even have topographical maps downloaded into
them for viewing on a screen and many allow you to record "way points" so you
can find your way back. It is being advertised as the greatest navigational tool
available, but, while they can be useful, you shouldn't throw away your map and
compass just yet.

First, while they can tell you your current position, do you know where
that latitude and longitude is? If you happen to have a radio and can call your
coordinates in to a rescue team, they will be able to find your exact position.
If you don't have a radio, you really need a map to determine where you are
located in the wilderness in which you are lost. They can give you coordinates
to hike out, but without a topographical map, you might be directed towards an
unpassable mountain ledge or a physical barrier like water. Only a map can tell
you what is ahead. A "Caution" section in the manual for the unit I use states:
"It is the user's responsibility to use this product prudently. This product is
intended to be used only as a travel aid and must not be used for any purpose
requiring precise measurement of direction, distance, location or topography." In
addition, they are not easy to use, and it takes practice to become really familiar
with them.

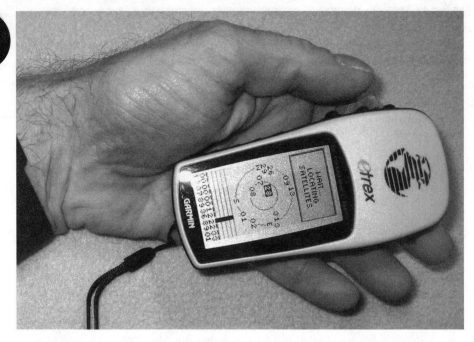

The author's Garmin eTrex GPS unit showing size and screen.

Did I mention they run on batteries? The model I have, a Garmin eTrex, runs for only 22 hours in battery-saver mode (less than one day!), and this time is significantly reduced if you use the backlight mode (needed at night). This necessitates that I carry extra batteries if I want to use it for any length of time. I have never had a map or compass stop working because of dead batteries. Also, it is a precision electronic instrument and can be easily broken, and although it is water resistant, it is not waterproof. You should also be aware of the fact that although they are not affected by weather or cloud cover, they don't work well, or at all, under a heavy overhead canopy. I have had problems getting a signal under heavy vegetation, and I can't always find an open field. There are some places in the Adirondacks where I also cannot get a signal for whatever reason.

I'm not trying to bash GPS units. I'm just trying to inform you of some of their shortcomings. A GPS unit can be a great supplementary tool for navigation, or as a compliment to a radio, but don't make it your "primary" or "only" navigational tool.

FAST FACTS:

Each of the 3,000 to 4,000-pound solar-powered GPS satellites circle the globe about 12,000 miles above the surface, making two complete rotations every day. The orbits are arranged so that at any time, anywhere on Earth, there are at least four satellites "visible" in the sky.

The author's pace beads have five beads at the top and nine beads at the bottom.

PACE BEADS

Pace beads are not a primary navigational tool, but rather a supplemental one. They are used to count your paces so you will have a general idea of how far you have traveled. First of all, you have to know the distance of your pace (each time the same foot hits the ground). Once you know this distance, you can count them and calculate the general distance you have traveled (keep in mind the distance of your pace can differ when going up or down hills, walking in snow, etc.). Military units measure distances in meters, and this can also be calculated, but I like to use feet so I can easily determine miles traveled.

Pace beads usually have four or five beads at the top and nine beads at the bottom. If you know your pace is approximately 5 feet, you know that for every 100 paces, you travel approximately 500 feet. So every 100 paces, you pull down one of the beads from the nine-bead group. After all nine have been pulled down and after the next 100 feet, you pull down a bead from the four- or five-bead group, which means you have traveled approximately 5000 feet (a mile is 5280 feet). You then pull the nine-bead group back up and start over. After the next 5000 feet, you pull down another bead from the four- or five-bead group, and you have now traveled 10,000 feet. You continue in this manner, pulling the nine-bead group back up when they are depleted. When the four- or five-bead group is depleted, and you have traveled 20,000 to 25,000 feet, start over with all beads.

While pace beads only provide you with a general or approximate distance, they can help you determine approximately how far you have traveled. If your map indicates that a body of water lies 2 miles ahead and you have traveled 3 to 4 miles without seeing it, you know you are probably not traveling in the right direction.

As you can see, the components for navigation are not very complex. If all else fails, at least have a compass in your survival kit.

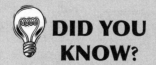

DID YOU KNOW?

The old saying about using moss on a tree to indicate north is not accurate because moss grows completely around some trees. Actually, growth is more lush on the side of the tree facing the south in the Northern Hemisphere and vice versa in the Southern Hemisphere.

WATER PURIFICATION

CHAPTER 5
WATER & FOOD

You will learn in any good survival school that the human body needs water to remain functioning normally, and to survive. Without water, dehydration will set in, and your chances of survival will diminish quickly. There are various ways to collect water in the field, and this will also be taught in a good survival course. However, you cannot just collect water and drink it. While most water appears clear and clean (at least sometimes), you must consider all water contaminated. To avoid infesting your body with parasites – the last thing you need in a survival situation – you need to purify any water you drink.

Although not as important as water, food is also essential to keep the human body functioning. You can exist many more days without food than you can water, but if you are out there long enough, food will eventually be required.

This chapter will discuss those components of a survival kit that will provide you with purified water and food. You should carry as many of these components as your kit size allows.

WATER PURIFICATION

Without carrying anything in your kit, water can be purified by boiling it. Of course, this assumes you have the means to make fire and have a container to boil it in. It is better to carry a means to purify water, which requires less energy in an emergency situation.

The first option is iodine tablets, which make questionable water bacterially safe to drink. A major brand of iodine tablets is Potable Aqua, which is manufactured by WPC Brands, Inc. and is available at most camping and sporting goods stores. There are 50 tablets in each small glass bottle (2 inches tall x 1 inch in diameter). If this is too big for your kit, Exploration Products sells a small glass vial with a Teflon screw cap (necessary for re-packaging iodine tablets) that measures only 1-3/8 inches tall x 5/8 inch diameter. It only holds half as much but is great for mini kits. It should be noted that the original research to locate this small vial was conducted by Doug Ritter from the Equipped To Survive Foundation, Inc., and he certainly deserves the credit. Two tablets treat 1 quart or 1 liter of water. Directions are printed on the label.

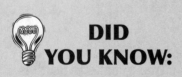

DID YOU KNOW:

It is estimated by some that as much as 90 % of the world's freshwater is contaminated.

Another iodine purification option is Polar Pure by Polar Equipment. Although larger than Potable Aqua (3 inches tall x 1-5/8 inches in diameter), it is handy if the space is available. To use, you simply fill the bottle with questionable water and shake. There are iodine crystals in the bottle and in one hour you have an iodine solution for purifying water (and the solution can be carried in the bottle so it is ready when

From left to right, Potable Aqua, a small re-packaging vial (with a dime for scale), Polar Pure, Aquamira and the recently introduced Micropur in foil packets.

you need it). There is a thermometer built into the side of the bottle with directions to indicate how many capfuls of the iodine solution to use per quart or liter of water, depending on the temperature. Also, the bottle is manufactured with an insert that prevents the iodine crystals from falling out of the bottle when pouring out the iodine solution. It will purify up to 2000 quarts of water and is available at many camping stores such as Eastern Mountain Sports and Campmor.

Although I prefer iodine-based purification, there are also chlorine-based purification treatments. One of these is Aquamira, manufactured by McNett Corporation. This is a two-part system with each part contained in a 1-inch x 1-inch square plastic bottle 3-3/16 inches high. One bottle also has a mixing cap on top. To use, you place seven drops from each bottle in the mixing cap and let stand for 5 minutes. You then fill a container with 1 quart or 1 liter of water and add the mixture from the cap. After shaking or stirring and letting stand for 15 minutes (30 minutes if the water is very cold or turbid), the water is now purified and ready to drink. Aquamira is available from most stores that sell Potable Aqua and Polar Pure.

A recent addition to chlorine-based purification is Micropur by Katadyn, which also manufactures many water purifiers (see next section). This system uses one tablet per liter of water. Each tablet is in a foil capsule with 10 capsules per sheet, three sheets per package (30 tablets total per package). Although I have not yet personally used this product, I find the fact that individual foil capsules can be cut off the sheet and placed in a flat mini kit a possible advantage to small bottles. It is available from the above-mentioned stores.

WATER FILTERS

Most water filters only filter water; they do not purify it. And although there are some units that both filter and purify, most do not. Depending on the size of the filter (and you must check before buying), a filter will eliminate protozoa (such as *Giardia* and *Cryptosporidium*) and most bacteria. They will not eliminate viruses or bacteria smaller than the size listed on the filter (normally 0.2 – 0.3 microns). Most water filters are too large for most mini or small survival kits and will only fit in larger kits. I find purification the best option, but water filters can filter considerable water in a short time, and if in doubt, you can always purify the water after filtering it. They are also handy for filtering dirty water before purification.

One unit that is fairly small (good for a survival pack or large kit) is the Katadyn Hiker. It uses a paper-type filter and pumps a good amount of water rapidly. I have used this on various survival trips and it is easy to use.

From left to right, this photo shows the Hiker, MSR Miniworks and the Frontier filter.

Another filter I have used is the MSR Miniworks, which is a ceramic filter-based system. It is designed so a wide-mouth Nalgene water bottle can screw to the bottom, which eliminates the need for a second hose. I thought this was a nice feature, but it does not pump as fast as the Hiker.

A new introduction in water filters, the Frontier Filter by McNett Corporation is a small filter (3-7/8 inches long x 1 inch in diameter). A small plastic straw (included) attaches to the filter, and the filter body is inserted directly into water, with care taken not to submerge or otherwise contaminate the straw. You then drink directly from the straw. It is small enough to be carried in a small kit and looks promising. I have not used it yet (although I just purchased it), but plan on experimenting with it this coming season.

Again, keep in mind that most filters only filter water. If the product you buy does not specifically state that it both filters and purifies, then it only filters. Filters are nice items, but when in doubt, purify water by boiling or via a chemical treatment.

WATER CONTAINERS

All survival kits should provide a container, or some means, to hold water. A recommendation often made is to carry a non-lubricated condom. It is small (can even be carried in a mini kit) and can hold a considerable amount of water if supported in a sock, sleeve or trouser leg. I carried one or more in my kits for years.

I kept looking, however, for something that would pack very small, was durable, and could be used for other purposes. After watching my wife use an oven bag for baking a turkey (Reynolds Oven Bag), I started playing with it. It is constructed of a Mylar-type material and is very durable. I have filled them with several quarts of water and spun them around my head and actually hit them up against the wall in the shower (these are times my wife just shakes her head). For mini kits, I cut them down to half their height, although a full bag folds down to a very small size. I fill each bag that I have cut down with 1 quart of water and hold it up. I then draw a horizontal line on the outside with a small permanent marker indicating 1 quart. When I need to use the bag to purify water, I fill it to that point and automatically know how many purification tablets to use. For bags that I don't cut down, I also put marks at the 2- and 3-quart locations.

As a multi-purpose component, this oven bag can also be used to store several quarts of water that is already purified (even if the water has been boiled, you can pour it directly into the bag without hurting it, as it is an oven bag made to withstand extreme heat). It can be used to collect water by means of transpiration from plant vegetation (this is taught in most survival courses) and can be used as a waterproof container to protect equipment or supplies (I always carry some twist ties, which are supplied with the oven bags, to secure the tops of the bags).

A useful commercially available water bag is the "Water Bag" sold by Exploration Products. It is a lightweight, durable 2-gallon bag made from PVC. It has a built-in carry handle, and because of the design of the pour spout, it folds completely flat when empty. I carry one or more of these in all my medium and large kits.

Another valuable item to carry in a survival kit is zip-lock bags. I never liked the way they folded because of the "zip-lock" aspect, but for medium to large kits, they can be used as a water container as well as for other uses. They are not as durable as oven bags, so you can't be banging them around.

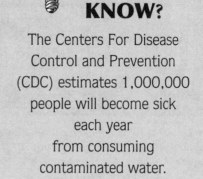

DID YOU KNOW?

The Centers For Disease Control and Prevention (CDC) estimates 1,000,000 people will become sick each year from consuming contaminated water.

The above water containers are fine for mini and small kits. However, if you are going to build medium to large kits, you should have more substantial containers for carrying water. These would include flexible canteens, bladder hydration systems, hard water bottles and canteens.

Let's start with flexible canteens, which are manufactured by various companies such as Nalgene and Platypus. They are made from a clear flexible plastic laminate that allow them to be folded or rolled up when not in use. They come in various sizes, including one that is designed to fit in the leg pocket of BDU (Battle Dress Utilities) trousers. They can be carried rolled or folded in a kit for use when needed, or carried filled and then rolled or folded for storage to reduce size. They have leak-proof caps, and some have gusseted bottoms, so they will stand up when filled. Also, most can be frozen and some can even be boiled. These flexible canteens are available with small-mouth and large-mouth openings, which is often a

The size of folded oven bags in relation to a condom package. The center bag is a full-size bag (about twice the height of a condom), and the bag on the right is cut in half, which when compressed, is actually smaller than the condom.

WATER CONTAINERS

The left photo shows a full-size Reynolds Oven Bag (large) and one that has been cut in half so it will fold smaller for a mini kit. The full bag will hold over 2 gallons and the half bag over 1 gallon. The right photo shows the 1-quart marking the author places on the oven bag with a permanent marker.

Two views of the commercial "Water Bag" from Exploration Products – unfolded on the left and folded and placed into a small belt-size survival kit on the right.

trade-off, as the small mouth packs better, but the wide mouth is easier to fill. They can be purchased at most camp and sports stores.

Another type of water container that has been introduced in recent years is the Hydration System. It is basically a flexible water reservoir (or bladder) contained in some type of carrier for protection. It has a long tube that hangs out with a drinking valve (most have to be bitten when drinking, so the water does not run out when not in use). Many are now being offered in some type of mini backpack or fanny pack. You could build your survival kit directly into these types of containers.

This type of hydration system is being manufactured by various companies, with one of the originals being Camelbak. They make many different designs, from small hydration fanny packs to small, medium and large hydration backpacks. Another company that makes various-size designs is Blackhawk – they call their product HydraStorm – and their units are geared

FAST FACTS:

Each day humans must replace 2.4 liters of water, some through drinking and the rest taken by the body from foods eaten.

more for the military. There are other manufacturers, such as Gregory, who are also offering these type units.

I personally don't prefer a bladder-type hydration system, as I find them hard to fill in the field. However, many people are going this way. You will have to experiment with them and decide for yourself if they are adequate for your survival kit needs.

Some medium-size survival kits can be built into a fanny pack, which often provides room on the ends for water bottles, and larger kits can be built into the backpacks. Of course, this also allows you to start out with a quantity of water.

You could always carry the type of water bottle you buy at a store, but I find they are not very sturdy and tend to break after continued use. There are various types of water bottles designed for outdoor use available on the market. One of these, the Nalgene water bottle, is made from Lexan and is unbreakable, leak-proof and available in many sizes. Able to be carried in various-sized medium to large kits, these bottles are available from most sporting goods and camping stores.

There are also 2-quart plastic military canteens, which are very durable. The metal type is no longer available (except at some military surplus shops), but is

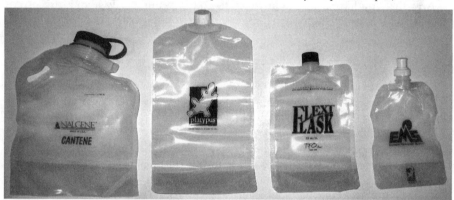

The above flexible canteens, from left to right, are 96-ounce, 2-liter, 32-ounce and 16-ounce capacities.

A view, from left to right, of a Platypus hydration unit without a pack, a Camelbak shoulder unit, a Gregory mini-pack unit and a Blackhawk HydraStorm unit.

SNARES / SNARE WIRE

Shown above, from left to right, are 32-ounce wide-mouth, 16-ounce narrow-mouth and 14-ounce wide-mouth Nalgene water bottles followed by 2-quart plastic and 2-quart metal U.S. military canteens.

what I carry during the winter months. They can be placed into a fire if your water freezes and can also double as a foot warmer in a sleeping bag.

Now that you have a means in which to collect water, purify it and carry it, we will take a look at the components necessary for you to obtain food, or carry it with you.

SNARES AND/OR SNARE WIRE

Some people may be offended by the thought of catching small animals and eating them for food, but in an emergency situation, you would be surprised at what you will do (and eat!). All survival kits should have ready-made snares or provide the ability to make them.

In my opinion, the best commercially made snare is the Thompson Survival Snare, which has been used since WWII in the survival kits of the U.S. armed forces. Two sizes are provided in the "Thompson Survival Snare Kit." The smaller is for small rabbits, birds and other similar-size animals. The larger snare is for muskrat, mink, large rabbits, skunk and other similar-size animals. These are self-locking steel snares and come complete with tie line and instructions and illustrations. Available from Brigade Quartermaster and Exploration Products, they are good for medium to large kits but are too big for mini kits.

For a mini kit, and some smaller kits, you need to carry wire that is appropriate for making snares. I recommend carrying 24-gauge brass or galvanized wire (I prefer brass). You should carry as much as is practical for the kit you are building but at least 10-20 feet. You will also learn in Chapter 9 that this wire is another one of those "multi-purpose" components that has other uses, so carry as much as you can.

Another option for making a snare is steel fishing leaders, which you will learn more about under the next heading. They can adequately be used as snares in a survival situation.

Although snares are indeed a means in which to obtain food in an emergency situation, you need to put out a good quantity in hopes of catching an animal. You do need training (again, a good survival school will teach this skill), as there are specific places and configurations in which to set them in order to be somewhat successful. However, if you are near water, especially fresh water, there is another way to catch food, and it can be done at the same time your snares are working for you.

Fishing Kits

Fishing is a good way to obtain food in a survival situation, but in order to be successful, you have to be equipped. A survival school can show you how to make some fishing tackle in the field, but you will expend much less energy if you have the basics with you. For this reason, every survival kit should have some type of a fishing kit. Even a mini kit should have the basics for fishing.

In my opinion, the basic fishing tackle that should be carried in a mini survival kit consists of at least 12 assorted hooks, six swivels and six split shot. My fishing kit for my survival tin has exactly this amount of tackle in a small tube, 1-3/16 inches tall x 7/16 inch in diameter. I have a slightly larger kit that has 14 assorted hooks, six swivels, six split shot and one small lure.

An even larger fishing kit, which fits into a small survival kit that I carry on my belt, is packaged in a "mini" Altoids tin and holds two dozen assorted hooks, one large hook to use as a gaff, one dozen snap swivels, 34 split shot (overkill, but they fit so nicely in a mini bottle that holds them in the tin), two mini Daredevle spoons, aluminum foil (for making lures) and 100 feet of 12-lb line. This kit measures 2-3/8 inches long x 1-1/2 inches wide x 5/8 inch thick (and it could be smaller if not for the bottle of split shot).

Another kit I made is inside a piece of plastic PVC pipe that is 5/8 inch in diameter by 4 inches long. This hangs off my medium-size survival kit. I threaded the top of the pipe and used an old brass fitting to seal one end. I also filed the piece that stuck out so it would provide me with a small hole to place a split ring and mini snap link (to attach it to a kit or pack). I ground down two areas on the outside of the pipe approximately 3/4 inch wide by 1/16 inch deep, being careful not to go through the wall of the plastic pipe, and wound 50 feet of 12-lb line around the pipe in one of these areas and 50 feet of 24-lb line in the other. I marked each with permanent marker and used electrician's tape to hold them in place. I then made a smaller clear plastic tube that would fit inside the pipe, which has end caps. Inside this smaller tube, I put the tackle kit consisting of hooks, swivels, a mini Daredevle spoon and split shot. Once this tube slides inside the pipe, a rubber end cap holds it inside.

You should also carry at least 50 feet of 12- to 20-pound-test fishing line. I prefer it be wound around something so it can be carried in a small place. For my

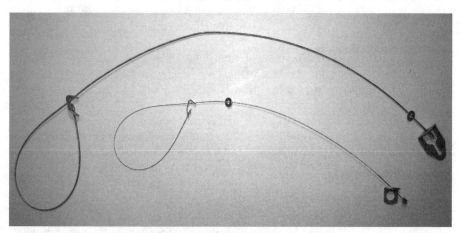

The above photo is a view of the Thompson Survival Snares.

On the left side is a snare made from 24-gauge brass wire. On the right side is a snare made from a steel leader.

mini kits, I wind the fishing line around small plastic sewing-machine bobbins or on small plastic floss bobbins, depending on the configuration of the kit. I can get about 50 feet on sewing-machine bobbins and 100 feet on plastic floss bobbins. Keep in mind that you want to choose a fishing line that does not have "memory," so it will straighten out properly after being wound on a small holder. Some lines I have found effective for this purpose are Spiderwire original braid and PowerPro braided microfilament line. Both are green in color (which attracted my attention) and are very strong.

For medium to large survival kits, you can, of course, carry larger fishing kits with more tackle. You can even carry a small collapsible or break-down fishing rod if the space is available. I have a small plastic tackle box that folds in half and has multiple divided sections. It measures 3-3/4 inches long x 2-1/2 inches wide x 1-1/8 inches deep. It fits into a small pocket on the back of my survival pack and holds several dozen each of #10, #8, #6, and various other medium and large hooks. It also holds several dozen swivels and snap swivels, several dozen split shot, several lures and spoons, half dozen flies, and 50 feet of both 12-lb and 20-lb line. It is a very small package for what it holds.

For a large canoe survival kit, I made a small fishing kit that includes tackle, a small collapsible rod and a mini spin-cast reel. The tackle and rod fit into a plastic tube 1-7/8 inches in diameter x 12 inches long that has a screw-on cap on one end. The mini reel fits into a very small pouch that clips to the rod and tackle tube with a small snap-link.

If you don't really know anything about fishing, there are some survival fishing kits available commercially. The best I have seen, which are freshwater kits, are available from Exploration Products. They have a small kit and a large kit, both of which are designed for survival kits.

Another commercially available item that is used in many military survival kits – and is so effective that it is outlawed in the state of Minnesota – is called the SpeedHook. This device, like a mousetrap for fish, is spring-loaded and activates and sets the moment a fish takes the bait. No rod is required and it can be used over and over again. A handy device for any small or large kit, it can also be used as a snare to catch small animals.

A fishing yo-yo can also be a good item for a survival fishing kit. They are approximately the diameter of a donut and therefore only good for medium to large kits. Basically an automatic reel with a stainless-steel spring inside a disc, it has a

The top row of the above photo shows the author's small fishing kit built into a mini Altoids tin. The bottom row, from left to right, shows a mini fishing kit in a tube for a survival tin, a slightly larger tube kit, and the custom fishing kit built into a 5/8-inch diameter piece of plastic PVC pipe that holds the line and the insert tube that holds the tackle.

line attached to it so it can be tied to an overhanging limb, which suspends it over the water. There are several feet of nylon line wrapped around the spring. You dangle the end of the line in the water, after baiting the hook, and set the trigger mechanism on the side of the yo-yo. When a fish bites, the trigger is tripped, setting the hook. The reel then automatically reels in the fish.

A gill net is another good supplement to any medium to large survival kit. The one I use is 12 feet x 4 feet and is ideal for stretching across a stream or creek. You can hang it over water with the bottom weighted or string it between poles. It packs in a small zip-lock bag, 6 inches x 3-1/2 inches x 1-1/4 inches.

Cup Or Small Pot

All but the smallest survival kits should have some type of metal cup or pot. It can be used to collect water or purify water by boiling it over a fire. For smaller kits, you should carry aluminum foil, which can be used to fashion a cup to boil water and can be folded very flat for storage in a small kit.

Another useful item I now use in all my small kits is a mini loaf pan. They measure approximately 6-1/8 inches long x 3-3/4 inches wide x 2 inches high. I fold them flat by folding in the ends and then the sides. This makes a small package and several can be carried in a relatively small space.

For larger kits, you should carry an actual metal cup or small pot. There are many configurations available from camp stores. I prefer to use one that has been

EMERGENCY FOOD

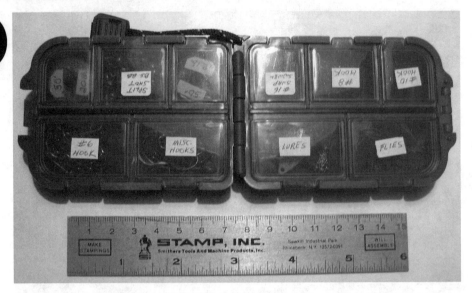

Fishing kit in small plastic tackle case that fits in author's survival pack.

designed to fit over the bottom of a water bottle or canteen. The water container is already taking up a certain amount of space in your kit, so use that same space for your cup or pot.

The Alpine, a 16-ounce stainless-steel cup with handles that fold flat against the sides, is designed to fit over a 1-quart Nalgene bottle. The Mini Solo Cook Kit is a complete pot-and-cup set made by Snow Peak. The pot fits over a 1-quart Nalgene bottle and the cup fits over the pot. The handles fold flat against the side, and it is available in both aluminum and titanium. I have the titanium set and it only weighs 5.5 ounces (it is rather expensive, however). Both of these cups and pots are available at Campmor, a large camping store in Saddle River, New Jersey.

Another cup made for the government is the military canteen cup. It fits over the 1-quart military canteen. The newer model has handles that fold against the sides, but I prefer the older model, which has a handle that folds under the cup. When unfolded and locked in position, the handle protrudes further from the cup, which keeps it cooler when cooking over a fire. The handle is also configured so you can extend it with a stick, keeping it even cooler when cooking. The newer cups are available from most military supply stores, such as Brigade Quartermasters and Ranger Joe's. The older model can only be found at military surplus stores.

EMERGENCY FOOD

When in a survival situation, you have to stay hydrated (water) and keep up your energy. You have already learned about various components that can assist you in obtaining food, but you should have something with you to make that food taste better, or at least provide you with a means of mental comfort. Obviously, with a mini kit, you won't have much room for emergency food. You should, however, carry some bouillon (either cubes or packets depending on the configuration of your kit), which can be used as a simple soup broth or to improve the taste of some of the things you might catch and cook. A couple of tea bags (or coffee bags) should be carried and can be a great morale builder on a cold rainy night. Sugar is

EMERGENCY FOOD

The left photo shows the author's fishing reel and case. The right photo shows the fishing rod, tackle tubes and small round tackle container, which all fit inside the black tube with screw-on cap that clips to a pack.

another item that can be carried in cube or packet form. It can be used with your hot drink or as an energy booster. Salt should also be carried if possible, as it helps those taste buds with certain foods, and it can replace salt loss due to dehydration. Some hard candy can fit in all but the smallest mini kits and can provide an energy, as well as a morale, boost.

Another item that can be carried in most kits is small foil packages of electrolyte and energy booster mixes. The first helps to replace electrolytes in the body much like some sports drinks do. The second, which I carry and use, is a super energy-boosting mix that includes 1000 mg of vitamin C, various mineral complexes and vitamins. Called Emer'gen-C, it not only tastes good but can also hide the taste of water that doesn't (such as water with iodine in it).

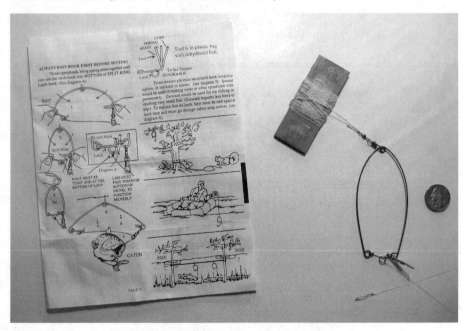

The SpeedHook with accompanying instruction booklet.

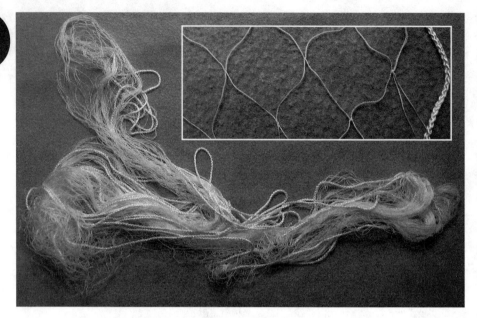

A gill net with an inset showing close-up view of net.

For all small and medium-size kits, you should carry some candy or energy bars. Of course, energy bars (there are hundreds to choose from) provide maximum calories (normally 180-260), but I haven't yet found one that tastes great. I prefer granola bars, as they taste good, are good for you, and don't melt in my kit. The one I carry is the Quaker Chewy Oatmeal Raisin. They only have 110 calories (about half of power bars), but they are only about half the size, and I can carry almost two for one. This is one choice you will have to make, but a good rule is to carry as many as you can fit.

 DID YOU KNOW?

1. Despite what many fishermen think, most fish are actually colorblind. Fish CAN see color shadings, reflected light, shape and movement, which probably explains why they accept or reject certain artificial lures used by anglers.

2. There is very little salt in most fish. In fact, more than 240 species contain so little salt that doctors recommend them in salt-free diets.

From left to right, a large cup made from 1-1/2 feet of aluminum foil, a 3-foot piece of aluminum folded to show its small size, a mini loaf pan, the first fold of that pan, and then the finished pan flat and ready to pack in your kit.

Make sure that your emergency food is in a kit that is waterproof, or package it in a small waterproof container or zip-lock bag. I use a vacuum sealer to seal these small items, which keeps them fresh as well as waterproof.

EMERGENCY RATIONS

Emergency food should be carried in every survival kit, except for maybe the smallest. However, if you carry a larger kit, such as a pack or vehicle kit, you will want to include emergency rations. These will provide you with more calories and will sustain you for a longer period of time without having to collect food.

The first type is actually called "Emergency Food Rations," and the two main manufacturers are Survivor Industries and S.O.S. Food Lab. Survivor Industries' product, Mainstay Emergency Rations, is a foil-wrapped package (waterproof) containing six 16-ounce bars of 400 calories each for a total of 2400 calories. I carry this type (I always have a couple in my truck), and you would be surprised at how good the bars taste. The package measures 6 inches long x 3-1/2 inches wide x 1 inch thick. Mainstay Emergency Rations have a 5-year shelf life. I have not personally tried the S.O.S. Food Lab Emergency Food Rations, but I have heard they are also good and have 2000 calories per package. These types of rations are handy because they are waterproof (until opened), need no

The Alpine cup over a 1-quart Nalgene bottle (left), an older military canteen cup over a 1-quart military canteen (middle) and the Snow Peak titanium Mini Solo Cook Kit over a 1-quart Nalgene bottle (right).

EMERGENCY RATIONS

FAST FACTS:

What is a calorie? A calorie is a unit of energy. We tend to associate calories with food, but they apply to anything containing energy. For example, a gallon (about 4 liters) of gasoline contains about 31,000,000 calories. Specifically, a calorie is the amount of energy, or heat, it takes to raise the temperature of 1 gram of water 1 degree Celcius (1.8 degrees Fahrenheit).

preparation and are relatively small for a larger kit.

The second type of emergency rations is the military or civilian M.R.E. (Meal Ready to Eat). This is a complete food package that provides an entrée (such as beef stew, chicken & rice pilaf, chili w/macaroni, etc.), a side dish, a dessert, a cracker pack with a spread, a beverage base and condiment pack. The entrée can be eaten right out of the pouch without preparation, but they taste better if heated. The military version provides a heating device that you place in a separate pouch and add water and the entrée pouch. It automatically heats the entrée pouch. This perk is not included in any of the civilian versions. These rations have a shelf life of 3 to 5 years. M.R.E.s can be obtained from Brigade Quartermasters and other military suppliers, but only the civilian version is available. The heaters can still be obtained from Cheaper Than Dirt. These rations are suitable for large kits but are rather bulky. I find that if you carry only the entrée, they take up much less room (of course, this also means fewer calories).

The last type of emergency rations is the freeze-dried meal. Everyone's opinion is different, but I find that these taste the best (but they are bulky). They can be

At top left is a package of bouillon and three bouillon cubes. Below that are sugar packets, and on the bottom is a mini salt and pepper shaker. The center shows a couple of power bars with author's favorite granola bar at bottom. At the top right are electrolyte and power-drink mixes with coffee and tea bags shown below them.

From left to right, the Mainstay Emergency Ration, a complete M.R.E. package, an M.R.E. entrée and a freeze-dried meal package.

folded down to take up less space, but care should be taken to not break the seal. The biggest drawback is the need for water to re-hydrate them. I don't find this a problem because I usually can boil all the water I need. However, in a survival situation where water is scarce, they are not the best choice.

Whatever your choice, it makes sense to carry as many of these emergency rations as practical in large kits. Added to anything else I could find to eat, I have existed on one M.R.E. entrée per day for eight days.

 DID YOU KNOW?

Why freeze-dry? The basic idea is to completely remove water, while leaving the basic structure and composition of the material intact. There are two reasons someone might want to do this with food: • **1.) Removing water keeps food from spoiling for a long period of time.** Like people, microorganisms need water to survive, so if you remove water from food, it won't spoil. Enzymes also need water to react with food, so dehydrating food will also stop ripening. • **2.) Freeze-drying significantly reduces the total weight of food.** Most food is largely made up of water (in fact, many fruits are more than 80 to 90% water.) Removing this water makes food much lighter and easier to transport. Just five days of food can add approximately 10 pounds to a single kit or backpack.

EMERGENCY RATIONS

SMALL STOVES

SMALL STOVES

Although a small stove is not a necessity for a survival kit, it can be a useful item to have in an emergency situation. For obvious reasons, "the smaller the better" is a good rule to follow. The following stoves are either small or have a unique feature, making them ideal for survival situations.

The first stove will fit in most small survival kits and on up. Called the Esbit Folding Pocket Stove, it is very compact and measures only 3 inches x 4 inches x 3/4 inch and weighs 3-1/4 ounces. You could actually carry this stove in a shirt pocket, but let's put it in a survival kit. It has two locking positions for cooking: fully open for a large cup or pot, or an angled position for a small cup. In either position, it provides a stable support for cooking.

The Esbit stove runs on small solid-fuel tablets that are individually sealed in airtight plastic and foil-formed packets. They come three per strip, and each tablet

The small size of the Esbit stove is shown here (left). The stove can be used in the angled cook position (center) or in the fully open position (right), which also shows the 4 solid-fuel tablets stored inside (only one tablet is used at a time).

Above is the Pocket Cooker in the closed position while the right photo shows it in the open position with the side door propped open for feeding it fuel (any small sticks, bark, etc.).

On the left is the optional pot set that the entire Sierra Stove fits into when disassembled. On the right, the stove is assembled with the battery box and switch.

From left to right, the author's drinking tube, assembled snow-melting stove, the wooden snow scoop and all of it packaged in a small stuff sack.

burns for approximately 15 minutes. You can store four tablets inside the stove when it is folded down in the carry position. I carry this stove in my day-trip kits and as a backup in larger kits. It does pack very nicely in the smallest of spots but is limited to the amount of fuel you carry. Manufactured by MPI Outdoors, it is available at most camping stores. They only cost about $9.99, so you can buy one for each kit.

The Pocket Cooker, which is a remake of an old Israeli military field stove, is a folding wood-burning stove that will fit in most medium to large kits, and if you have access to small bits of wood, bark, etc., you have a stove. Folded, it measures

The left photo shows the riveted stand-offs in the bottom (old top) of the paint can. Above, from left to right, is the paint can stove, Nuwick44 candle, the coffee-can pot and the MSR tea pot lid.

6-1/2 inches long x 3-3/4 inches wide x 7/8 inch thick. It is easily assembled, and there are no parts to lose, as it is all connected together. It takes a little practice folding it back up, but once you get it, it's easy. It is manufactured by Innovative Products, Inc. and can be purchased for $19.95 at www.firstinnovativestove.com.

Another stove for larger and/or vehicle kits is the Sierra Stove, a wood burner with a fan built in the base. A battery box holds one AA battery and has a switch with two positions: low and high. A wire attaches this small box to the base, which snaps into the bottom of the actual stove and which stores inside the stove when packed. When the fan is on, the fire roars, and it actually reminds you of a mini forge. It burns small pieces of wood, twigs, bark, pinecones, etc. While the stove works adequately under certain conditions, I have mixed feelings about it, as it does have some shortcomings for field use. The fan in the base is open and should have some type of wind block. Also, the battery box is not waterproof (nor is the fan) and therefore there are potential problems when it rains. Lastly, the battery does not like to work when really cold, so this is definitely not a winter stove. Manufactured by ZZ Manufacturing, Inc., it measures 6-1/4 inches high (4 inches high when the base is stored inside the stove) x 5 inches in diameter. An optional pot set is available that will store the entire stove, base and battery box inside.

The last survival stove is an emergency snow-melting stove that I made for carrying in the winter. As long as you have snow, you have drinking water. However, I needed a quick way to melt snow without having to make a fire.

I wanted to design a stove for melting snow that used a Nuwick44 candle as the heat source. After playing with the Nuwick44 (see Chapter 2) and various-sized cans, I found, to my surprise, that the lid groove of a 1-quart paint can fit perfectly over the lip of the candle. I wanted the paint can to sit directly on top of the candle so the lip of the candle sat up into the lid groove of the paint can, which meant the paint can had to sit upside down on the candle. I cut the bottom out of the paint can with a can opener, and the bottom of the can now became the top of the stove. In order to provide oxygen to the candle flames, I cut two rows of 3/8-inch holes around one-fourth of one side of the can where it sat on the candle before repeating the holes on one-fourth of the opposite side. With the holes on only two sides, I can turn one of the two sides that doesn't have holes towards the wind, blocking it from the flame.

			Ease of	Coaling		
Species	**Heat**	**Lbs./cord**	**Lighting**	**Qualities**	**Sparks**	**Fragrance**
Alder	Med-Low	2540	Fair	Good	Moderate	Slight
Apple	High-Med	4400	Difficult	Excellent	Few	Excellent
Ash	High	3440	Fairly diff.	Good-Exc.	Few	Slight
Beech	High	3760	Difficult	Excellent	Few	Good
Birch (White)	Med	3040	Easy	Good	Moderate	Slight
Cherry	Med	2060	Difficult	Excellent	Few	Excellent
Elm	High	2260	Very diff.	Good	Very Few	Fair
Hickory	Very High	4240	Fairly diff.	Excellent	Moderate	Excellent
Ironwood	Very High	4000	Very diff.	Excellent	Few	Slight
Locust (Black)	Very High	3840	Difficult	Excellent	Very Few	Slight
Madrone	High	4320	Difficult	Excellent	Very Few	Slight
Maple (Red)	High-Med	3200	Fairly diff.	Excellent	Few	Good
Maple (Sugar)	High	3680	Difficult	Excellent	Few	Good
Mesquite	Very High	N/A	Very diff.	Excellent	Few	Excellent
Oak (Live)	Very High	4600	Very diff.	Excellent	Few	Fair
Oak (Red)	High	3680	Difficult	Excellent	Few	Fair
Oak (White)	Very High	4200	Difficult	Excellent	Few	Fair
Pecan	High	N/A	Fairly diff.	Good	Few	Good
Walnut	High-Med	N/A	Fairly diff.	Good	Few	Fair

Fast Facts: Wood Heat & Cooking Guide

SMALL STOVES

Now that I had a stove, I needed a melting pot. I found, again to my surprise, that a 1-pound coffee can (of course, it is not really 1 pound in today's world) fit inside the 1-quart paint can with the bottom cut out. Since it was easy to obtain, and replace, I went with the coffee can. However, when I slid the coffee can down into the paint can, it sat completely down on the bottom (the old top) of the paint can, blocking the ventilation holes and putting out the flames. To hold the coffee can up above the ventilation holes, I used four pop rivets evenly spaced, 1 inch up from the bottom of the stove. Before I squeezed the rivets, I put a small stand-off (a small aluminum tube) approximately 1/4 inch long over the rivet. When the rivet was squeezed, it left a 1/4-inch stand-off inside the stove. The four of these kept the coffee can from sliding down past the ventilation holes when placed inside the stove. I now had a snow-melting stove for the cost of a couple of cans.

While trying to devise a lid for the coffee can – so the snow would melt faster – I found a ready-made lid from an old MSR tea pot. Just when I thought my luck would run out, I found that the Nuwick44 candles slid perfectly down inside the coffee can for storage, and that it would hold three. I added a cut-down wooden spoon as a snow scoop and a length of plastic tubing so I could start drinking the water as soon as the snow started melting. I now always carry this stove when snowshoeing.

CHAPTER 6

SHELTER & PROTECTION

Shelter and protection are extremely important components of a survival kit. In a survival situation, you can quickly become incapacitated by the elements. This could include hyperthermia (heat that causes your body temperature to rise above 98.6° F) or hypothermia (cold that causes your body temperature to drop below 98.6° F). If your body enters either of these conditions, your mental and physical abilities diminish rapidly, and your chances of building a fire, signaling, navigating, etc. are drastically reduced. The same is true if you get severe sunburn or are swollen from unrelenting insect bites. Although not as debilitating as the above conditions, these still impede your ability to think clearly, which is why shelter and personal protection are of major importance. The following components will allow you to protect yourself from these types of conditions.

SURVIVAL BLANKETS

A survival blanket has so many uses it should be listed under "Multi-Purpose" items. There are various size survival blankets, and they can accommodate all but the most mini kit. The first is a small blanket called an Emergency or Space blanket. Made of a Mylar plastic film with aluminum coating on one side, they fold up extremely small (at least when you buy them – but you never can quite get them back to that small size after you use them) and store almost anywhere. The aluminum on one side of the blanket allows it to reflect warmth, which makes it possible for it to be used as a virtual heat regulator in various situations. In a cold environment, you can wrap the blanket around you with the aluminum side towards your body. This will reflect your body heat back towards you. In a hot environment, you can use the aluminum side facing out to reflect the sun's heat away from you.

Although they are small (the Emergency blanket is 52 inches x 82.5 inches and the Space blanket is 56 inches x 84 inches), survival blankets can also be used to make an emergency shelter. I have used them inside a lean-to-type shelter to reflect the heat from a fire onto my back. However, they are very thin and rip easily, so care should be taken when using them.

Using the reflective side, survival blankets can double as a signaling device. As a little tip, if you hold one of these blankets up to your eye, you will notice that you can see through them. In a situation where sunglasses are needed, such as bright sun on snow or water, you can tear off a small strip of your blanket and tie it around your head and over your eyes (reflective side out). You now have survival sunglasses.

The Original Space Blanket is a product of MPI Outdoors, and the Emergency Blanket is manufactured by Survivor Industries. Both of these are good. There are various other companies now manufacturing emergency blankets, but be careful and don't buy the cheapest you can find, as they are not all created equal.

From left to right, the Space Emergency Blanket, the Survivor Industries Emergency Blanket, the same blanket after trying to refold it and the Survivor Industries Cocoon.

Another survival blanket made from this type of material is the Heatsheet manufactured by Adventure Medical Kits. However, this blanket is a two-person emergency blanket and measures 59 inches x 96 inches. It also has a large bright orange stripe on one side for signaling, with survival and first-aid instructions printed directly on the orange stripe. The larger size is nice (again, size counts), but it does not pack as small. However, if you have room, it is a nice item to have with you.

Both MPI Outdoors and Survivor Industries also make an emergency bag out of this same material. The MPI version is the Space Emergency Bag, and Survivor Industries labeled theirs the Cocoon. They are both basically emergency sleeping bags that you can crawl into for full body coverage. Keep in mind the material is thin so don't thrash around in them.

Another type of survival blanket that is becoming popular is also made by Adventure Medical Kits. Made from Thermo-Lite, it is more substantial than the Mylar blankets and lasts longer after repeated folding (but it is also more bulky). The edges of the blanket are reinforced with waterproof binding tape. Again, they print survival and first-aid instructions on a bright orange stripe on one side. It measures 59 inches x 84 inches and is more durable for frequent usage.

The same company also makes the Thermo-Lite Emergency Bivvy Sack.

 **FAST FACTS:**

About 70 percent of winter storm deaths occur in automobiles. The rest are primarily due to heart attacks from overexertions such as shoveling heavy snow or from hypothermia caused by overexposure to cold. About 50 percent of deaths caused by exposure to cold (hypothermia) are to people over 60 years of age. Over 75 percent of these deaths are to men.

Starting from the left, the Adventure Medical Kits Thermo-Lite Emergency Blanket, the Thermo-Lite Emergency Bivvy Sack and the Space All Weather Blanket, all folded to show comparative size.

This is a survival sleeping bag that has a foot vent and a large opening (so you don't have to slide down into it) with Velcro closures. This is a neat little bag that measures 36 inches x 84 inches, and I have actually slept in it during summer outings. It comes in a bright yellow stuff sack and is ideal for medium and large kits.

The next type of survival blanket is the Space All Weather Blanket, a heavy-duty blanket measuring 60 inches x 84 inches. It is made from two layers of low-density polyethylene blended with vapor-deposited aluminum (it reminds you of the material of which small tarps are made). It is not as reflective as the thinner blankets, and it is only reflective on one side. The other side is all one color, and you have a choice of red, blue, orange or olive. It has reinforced corners with grommets and a vinyl binding around the entire outer edge. It is waterproof and can also be used as a ground cloth, shelter or signal flag (if you have a red or orange one). I have never gone on a wilderness outing without at least one of these blankets with me (that is, until the following was introduced).

MPI also makes the Space Sportsman's Blanket, which is identical to the All Weather Blanket with the addition of a hood on one side and hand inserts sewn into two corners so you can hold the blanket around you without exposing your hands to the weather. This is an ideal piece of equipment and folds just as small as the non-hooded blanket. I have used it as a reflector in front of a fire to reflect heat to my back, and it also makes a great windbreak for any wind coming at you from behind. I was surprised during a late fall outing – that turned into a cold, windy and rainy couple of days – just how much heat from a fire was reflected to my back, and entire body, just by holding the blanket open. The temperature inside the blanket was much warmer than the ambient temperature outside. My buddies called me Batman, but I was warm. If room is available, I never leave home without it.

No matter what size survival kit you decide on (excluding a mini), you should be able to find a survival blanket that will fit. Carry at least one, or one small and one medium or large, depending on the size of your kit. For shelter, warmth, signaling, rain protection, etc., they are an inexpensive form of protection.

PONCHOS OR RAIN GEAR

Our next concern is protection from the rain. This would include a poncho or other type of rain gear. There are various companies that manufacture emergency ponchos made of polyethylene and that pack very small. For small survival kits, this is about the only option. They are flimsy and rip easily, but they will protect you

The author using the Space Sportsman's Blanket as a reflector in front of a fire during an outing in the Adirondacks in the late fall. (Photo taken by Agnes Hall.)

from the rain, and having one is better than nothing. They only cost about $1.00 to $2.00 and are available at most camping and sports stores.

When most people think about ponchos, they think about the military poncho. I carried this type of poncho the entire time I was in the U.S. Marine Corps and, although bulky, it works. It can be used for rain protection, a waterproof ground cloth and, with the edge grommets, a shelter. They are made from ripstop nylon and are very durable. There are some civilian models available, but many are not the quality of the military one, so choose carefully.

Another poncho that is very durable, yet packs in less than half the size of

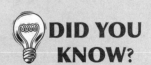

DID YOU KNOW?

Thunderclouds have an average life span of about one hour.

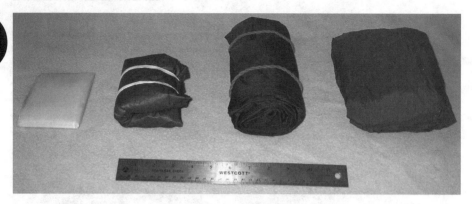

The comparative sizes of the emergency poncho, the Ultralite Poncho, the military poncho, and the Marmot rain jacket and trouser combination (from left to right).

the military poncho, is the Ultralite Poncho manufactured by Campmor. Made from 1.3-ounce silicone-impregnated ripstop nylon, which is extremely waterproof, compactable and lightweight, they are cut larger than most civilian ponchos and can be used additionally as a small shelter. The drawstring in the hood seals the head opening, and it has nylon web loops sewn in the corners for attaching with cord when used as a shelter. It also has reinforced rust-resistant snaps to close the sides to form wrist openings. It comes with a small mesh storage bag and will fit in all but mini and small kits. Campmor also offers an Extension Ultralite Poncho whereby they add 14 inches to the back so you can wear it over a pack without getting your lower back wet. The regular size costs $39.99 and the extended model $44.99. For my larger kits, I carry the regular Ultralite version as a backup to my regular rain gear and often end up using it as part of a shelter.

There are many types of civilian-designed ponchos and rain gear. The name of the game is size and most of them are bulky and hard to pack. I found an ideal rain suit manufactured by Marmot at Eastern Mountain Sports (EMS). It is a separate jacket and trouser (also sold separately) that folds down almost as small as the military poncho. A little pricey (about $112.00 for the jacket and $75.00 for the trousers), it is very durable and lightweight. I keep one set in my vehicle kit and one set in my pack. Keep in mind that you should pick rain gear that serves more than one purpose (as with all survival kit components). Therefore, I do not

FAST FACTS:

The most common error in making a shelter is to make it too large. A shelter must be large enough to protect you, but it must also be small enough to help contain your body heat and hold as much warmth in as possible, especially in cold climates.

The author's 10 x 12-foot Ultralite Backpacking Tarp over a Byer ultra-light Moskito hammock. Keep in mind this tarp packs down to fit in a stuff sack 5 inches in diameter x 6 inches long.

suggest you choose a rain suit over a poncho, as a poncho can be used for other purposes, as described above. In my larger kits, I carry the small Marmot rain suit, but I always accompany it with the Ultralite Poncho. In my smaller kits, I carry just the Ultralite Poncho.

TARPS

Most tarps, although rugged and waterproof, are just too big, heavy and awkward to be included in most survival kits. You see them set up in most campsites in sizes from small to "I wonder if I can cover the entire campsite and my camper" size. The only tarps I have found adequate for a survival kit, in both size and durability, are the Campmor Ultralite Backpacking Tarps. They are made from the same material as the Ultralite Poncho described earlier and are available in three sizes, 6 feet x 8 feet, 8 feet x 10 feet and 10 feet x 12 feet. They have grommets along the outside perimeter approximately every 2.5 feet and have lightweight ties on the center seam, for multiple pitching options. The smallest one fits in a 3-inch-diameter x 5-inch-long stuff sack and weighs 9.2 ounces, and the larger one (I haven't played with the medium size) fits in a stuff sack 5 inches in diameter x 6 inches long and weighs 19 ounces. They pack incredibly small.

Another manufacturer that is offering an ultra-lightweight tarp is GoLite. They offer a small tarp called the Cave 1 that is to be used as a shelter only, as it has sewn-in ends and peaks. It only weighs 14 ounces, without stakes. I haven't experimented with one yet, but plan to do so. The price is $159.00, so I'm in no hurry.

If you have room in your kit and want to supplement a heavy-duty survival blanket, an ultra-lightweight tarp may be the way to go.

TUBE TENTS

A tube tent is a lightweight emergency shelter that is sold by many camping stores. Basically a polyethylene tube, it can be set up as a tent by stringing a cord through the tube and tying the ends between two objects such as trees (you will learn how to improvise a tube tent with a multi-purpose component in Chapter 9). I have seen these as part of many commercially available survival kits. They are reasonably light but don't pack very small and are not very durable. However, in a survival situation, you use what you have.

PARACHUTE CORD

Parachute cord is something you cannot have enough of in a survival kit, as it is probably the best utility cord available for survival purposes. But what exactly is it? Parachute cord, also called 550 cord, is actually 550-pound test parachute

PARACHUTE CORD

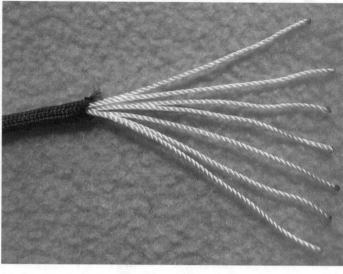

A small hank of the illustrious parachute cord, which is constructed of seven inner nylon lines.

shroud line used by the military. It is 1/8 inch in diameter and has a continuous filament nylon shroud with seven inner nylon lines. These inner nylon lines are also very strong and can be separated from the shroud for various uses such as sewing, fishing line, making nets, making snares, etc. If you had 25 feet of parachute cord with you and you separated the inner lines, you would have 175 feet of line available for survival use.

In order to separate the seven lines from the shroud, cut a short piece of shroud off each end (just enough to get by the melted part). Push back the shroud until you see the seven inner nylon lines. Hold onto the seven lines with one hand, without touching the shroud. Now hold the shroud on the other end, without grabbing the seven inner lines. With the hand holding the inner lines, pull them through the shroud, working slowly so you don't pucker the shroud, until the seven lines are completely out of the shroud. You now have seven individual nylon lines. But wait, there's more! If you needed very thin nylon lines for sewing or making a fine fishing line, each of the seven inner nylon lines can be un-twisted providing another three lines. These thin lines are really twisted but can be used individually. But wait, there's more! Don't throw away the empty shroud. It is very strong and can also be used for lashing. Keep in mind that separating the inner lines from the shroud is difficult with long pieces, so use only short pieces of cord, about 4 to 5 feet long.

It should be noted that although I indicated you should cut parachute cord for the purpose of removing the inner nylon lines, you should not cut it for other uses. The nylon shroud will continue to fray, revealing the inner lines. You don't want this for normal use. Therefore, you should always use a lighter to cut the cord, burning entirely through it, which melts the ends closed (sort of cauterizing the ends). Be very careful after doing this, as the ends will be very hot, and the melted nylon likes to stick to your fingers and continue burning (don't ask me how I know this; I just do). When I am not in the field, I use a small butane soldering iron with a hot-blade attachment, which cuts the cord nicely for those hanks I'm going to carry in my kits.

You should also be aware of the fact that "Not all parachute cord is created equal." There are various camp stores, etc. that sell "Para Cord," which sounds like parachute cord but is not the real thing. You can tell right away when you pull back the sheath and exclaim, "Where the hell are the seven inner lines?" Instead, you find a single bundle of some sort of fuzzy nylon that cannot be separated into individual lines. As they say, buyers beware!

Parachute cord is available in olive, black, tan and white, although white is sometimes hard to find. You can buy the real thing from Brigade Quartermasters in 50-foot, 100-foot, and 100-yard lengths and from Ranger Joe's. Please note that, although it has 550 pounds of tensile strength, parachute cord is not intended for rappelling or other life-supporting activities.

HEAD NETS

In any environment where bugs are a problem, you should carry a head net for protection. Available in various sizes and shapes, some head nets have large rings inside to hold them away from your face, but they do not pack very small. There are others, however, that have a spring steel band inside that folds down with a twist for storage, yet deploys when removed from the pouch. Brigade Quartermaster sells one like this attached to a soft-brimmed hat, and the whole thing folds up inside itself. It is called the Pop-Up Hat and Insect Headnet Combo.

I normally wear a brimmed hat, so it keeps a simple net off my face and neck. A head net I prefer, which packs down very small, is the Repel Deluxe Head Net. It has underarm loops that help keep it pulled down and tight to your clothing. It comes in a small net bag, which stays attached so you don't lose it, and is available from EMS and other camp stores at a cost of about $6.95.

HATS

A hat is essential for a survival kit. The type of hat depends on the environment. In areas where it is cold, you can prevent the loss of over half your body heat by wearing a hat. In a hot area, you need a brimmed hat to protect your head and neck from the sun. A staple for all but my mini kits is a simple skullcap, also known as a watch cap. Although wool is good, it does not pack very small, so I carry a polypropylene one instead (there are many tradeoffs in survival kit design). Another choice is a balaclava, which can be pulled completely down over the face and neck, with an oval hole for the eyes (or nose and mouth too). It can also be rolled up and worn as a skullcap (multi-functional – I like that).

For sun protection, you need a brimmed hat, yet you want the ability to pack it down small. There are various companies like Outdoor Research and EMS who make brimmed adventure hats from plain fabric to

DID YOU KNOW?

The head and neck can radiate as much as 60% of the body's heat production.

SUNGLASSES

The author's five-cord flat-braid hatband made from parachute cord is always available for survival use. Several fishhooks are under the 1-inch tubing that covers the sewn connection of the flat braid at right center of hat. Inside the hat, a Mini-Match and striker, aluminum foil and coil of fishing line can be found.

Gore-Tex (a waterproof material). They can be folded up and squished into a small area.

You will learn in Chapter 11 about selecting containers for a survival kit, but keep in mind that sometimes you have to think outside the box. The following is an example.

A hat can also be more than a hat. When I'm out in the field, I normally wear a waterproof hard-brimmed hat. A good friend and mentor of mine, Marty Simon, also wears a brimmed hat. I noticed when I first met him that he had a three-cord flat-braided hatband made from olive parachute cord. He said he made it so he would always have parachute cord on him. He also carried a couple of fishing hooks behind the braided band and a coil of fishing line inside the sweatband. Of course, my creative juices started to flow.

I wanted a wider band, so I used a five-cord flat-braided band from, of course, olive parachute cord. It not only looks better on my hat, but it provides me with almost twice the parachute cord. I used a piece of 1-inch olive nylon tubing to cover the area where the ends are sewn together. Behind that tubing, I have several fishhooks. Inside, I added a coil of fishing line, but I wanted more. I made a small pouch that would hold a Mini-Match and striker (see Chapter 2) and sewed the pouch into the rear of the inside of the hat. I also added a 1.5-foot piece of aluminum foil, folded lengthwise several times, so it would fit under the sweatband. I then waterproofed the areas where I sewed through the hat. I now had the means to make fire, purify water (making a cup with the aluminum foil and boiling the water over the fire) and collect food (fishing) in addition to the parachute cord for building a shelter and various other tasks. It just doesn't get any better than that!

SUNGLASSES

Sunglasses are an important personal protection item in most environments to protect from the sun's glare, especially in the snow or over water. Most are hard to pack, and they don't fold down very small. However, there is a solution for all but

The Emergency Sunglasses, open and folded.

the smallest kit. Disposable sunglasses are available from Exploration Products for about $1.00 a pair. They are lightweight, one-size-fits-all sunglasses that fold flat and store in an envelope. They are actually wrap-around glasses, so the sides of your eyes are protected also. I carry a pair of these in every one of my kits except my

FAST FACTS:

The Ultraviolet (UV) Index, developed in 1994 by the National Weather Service (NWS) and the US Environmental Protection Agency (EPA), helps Americans plan outdoor activities to avoid overexposure to UV radiation and thereby lower their risk to adverse health effects. EPA and NWS report the Index as a prediction of the UV intensity at noon, though the actual UV level rises and falls as the day progresses. Previously the Index was reported on a scale of 0 to 10+, with 0 representing "Minimal" and 10+ representing "Very High." The new global scale with revised exposure categories, now uses a scale of 1 (representing "Low") to 11 and higher (representing "Extreme").

Index Number	Exposure Level
< 2	Low
3-5	Moderate
6-7	High
8-10	Very High
11+	Extreme

SUNSCREEN / PERSONAL PROTECTION

mini and some specialty kits. And, even though they are called "disposable," they can be worn more than once. They even have adjustable cardboard temples.

SUNSCREEN

Protection from the sun also includes protection for your skin. Sunburn can be painful, and if burned bad enough, dangerous. Each kit (other than a mini) should include some sunscreen. The higher the SPF (Sun Protection Factor), the higher the protection. Choose an SPF of 15 or higher (I carry 30 or higher), making sure it offers both UVA and UVB protection and is waterproof and sweatproof. Sunscreen is available in small tubes and should fit in all but the smallest kit.

LIP BALM

Lip Balm is another personal protection item. It is sold in all drugstores and most grocery stores and weighs only ounces. Tuck one with an SPF rating in your kit somewhere.

BUG REPELLENT

For environments where bugs persist, bug repellent is a must. Available in a variety of brands, shapes and sizes, some well-known names include Ben's, Repel, Cutter, Sawyer, Natrapel, Muskol and Green Ban. The choice is yours, but keep the following in mind. DEET repels ticks, as well as insects, but there have been some medical warnings about it being toxic when absorbed by the bloodstream. It is not recommended for use by children, and adults should use it only for short periods. The tradeoff is protection versus absorption. I have used it in the past but found that if it leaks, it melts plastic (again, don't ask me how I know this). This bothers me, as it can destroy your gear and container (especially if your container is a pack or Cordura/nylon bag). I use an herbal insect repellent called Green Ban Double Strength, and it works for me but not for some others. Choose what works for you.

EXTRA CLOTHES

Extra clothes really depend on the size of your survival kit. Some kits will not accommodate anything beyond the absolute necessities. But the larger the kit, the more you can carry (and the less chance you will carry it). If you have room, always think multi-functional. If I have room for nothing else, I carry an extra pair of socks, which can also be used as gloves in cold weather or for protecting my hands when performing certain activities. If you want to carry a jacket, buy one of the lightweight models with the sleeves that zip off. Now you have a jacket and a vest. The same thing applies to trousers – lightweight with zip-off legs. Now you have extra trousers, shorts and swim trunks. I always wear a 1-3/4-inch-wide nylon-webbed belt made by SpecOps. Called the Better BDU Belt, it can be used as a tourniquet, a strap, lashing, for dragging small logs or even as a belt to hold up your pants. As always, think multi-functional.

CHAPTER 7
KNIVES & TOOLS

If I could only choose one item for a survival kit, it would be a knife. With a knife, I can make almost anything else I need in a survival situation. A discussion on knives is like a discussion on guns. It can be controversial and nobody will agree on the same thing. But, because of their importance, we must discuss the issue.

For all those who are "experts" on the subject of knives and their uses, I'm sure I'll receive some feedback. However, I don't recommend specific knives. I do recommend not carrying certain types of knives for survival purposes, and I do discuss the type of knives that are available, the pros and cons of certain knives, and the knives that work for me (but won't necessarily work for you). In other words, a knife is a very personal choice an individual must make for himself (or herself). Also, keep in mind that you may also make trade-offs in your choice of configuration or size, depending on the shape and size of your kit.

The following section will describe various types of knives and tools. The knife or tool with which you feel most comfortable, that works for you, and that gives you warm fuzzy feelings is the one you should choose and carry.

SOME BASICS

A survival knife should be made from high-carbon steel or hardened stainless steel. I prefer carbon steel for my main blade but have been known to carry stainless steel for supplemental blades. There are a multitude of blade types on the market. Some of them I don't suggest for survival purposes, such as tanto blades or double-edged blades (sometimes called daggers). These knives are designed primarily for self-defense and not for cutting wood, skinning or other survival requirements. The four blade types I suggest are pictured here.

Although all four of the blade types pictured are adequate for survival purposes, I suggest a drop-point or clip-point, as they are the most versatile. All of my knives are of these two types, but they are my choice. I know one logger who swears by a skinner. Again, what works best for you should dictate what type you carry.

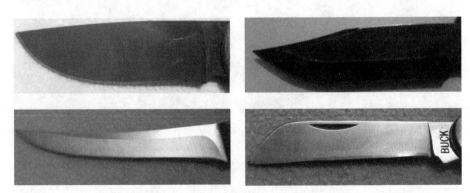

Clockwise from upper left are drop-point, clip-point, sheepfoot and skinner blades.

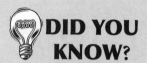

DID YOU KNOW?

Carbon is found in all types of steel and is the most important hardening element. High-carbon steel results when 0.5% or more carbon is present. Chromium, on the other hand, is added for wear resistance, hardness and corrosion resistance. In fact, a steel with at least 13% chromium is deemed "stainless steel."

My next suggestion is to buy well-known brands from reputable manufacturers who guarantee their knives. Some reputable manufacturers (and by all means, not all) are Becker, Browning, Buck, Camillus, Cold Steel, Columbia River, Gerber, Ka-Bar, Kershaw, Marbles, Ontario, Russell, Schrade, SOG, Timberline and Victorinox. Of course, there are many fine custom knife makers also, such as TOPS, Chris Reeve, Busse and Trace Rinaldi, to mention but a few.

The first question I am normally asked is, "Should I buy a fixed blade or folder?" There are arguments for both sides (and I mean arguments), but again the choice will ultimately be yours. I prefer a fixed-blade knife whenever possible. I like a fixed blade because, in my opinion, they are stronger. They have a full-length tang that continues to the butt end and have no moving parts. Although a folder is intrinsically weaker, it takes up less room and is easier to carry. However, if you do select a folder, make sure it has a blade lock, which keeps the blade from closing when you're using it. This option is often not available on many small folders or multi-function knives.

One last suggestion is to not buy a hollow-handle knife. There is a plethora of survival knives on the market based on the hollow-handle concept, where the

Knives from the author's collection that are of the types NOT recommended for survival use. The top two knives on the left are hollow-handled survival knives with the butt cap removed. The third knife down on the left appears to be a clip-point blade, but actually both the top and the bottom of the blade are sharpened, making it a double-edged knife. The three knives on the right are double-edged knives (daggers) that, while useful for self-defense purposes, are not recommended for survival.

FAST FACTS:

Blade Shapes (see photo page 69)

The clip-point blade, one of the most popular blade shapes, has a concave or straight cut-out at the tip (the "clip"), which makes the point sharper and lower for more control. It is found on many utility, hunting and camp knives.

The drop-point blade is another popular blade shape found on many hunting knives. The tip is lowered (dropped) via a convex arc from the spine. This provides greater control, which is important when field dressing an animal.

back of the handle screws off. This provides a round cavity for a small survival kit. Many even provide some VERY basic survival components. The problem with these knives is, at first glance, they appear to be a fixed-blade knife. They aren't. The blade is attached to the front of the tubular handle. This is where the weakness occurs. The knife blade will almost always break apart from the handle, leaving you with a blade and no handle. I have seen these at many flea markets in the $15 to $20 range. The price alone should suggest immediately that the knife is cheap (and I don't mean inexpensive), but people keep buying them. It is not until an emergency situation arises that you find out that the knife is junk.

RAZOR BLADES

A razor blade, or razor-knife blade, may not sound like a knife, but it is a cutting instrument and may be the only item that will fit in a mini kit. I don't recommend double-edged razor blades, as they are dangerous to handle, especially when you

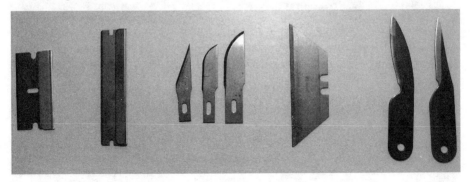

Here are a single-edged razor blade, a prep blade, three razor-knife blades, a utility knife blade and two Warren Cutlery carving blades (from left to right).

are trying to cut or whittle with them. Single-edged razor blades or single-edged razor-knife blades are the safest. A single-edged razor blade is normally available for safety razors in most drug or grocery stores. However, another single-edged razor blade that is good for a mini kit is a "prep blade" sold by most surgical supply houses. It is not as tall as a normal single-edged blade, but it is longer, giving you a little more control over the blade.

There are also small razor-knife blades such as those for Xacto knives. These come in various blade configurations. There are also utility knife blades, which are also single-edged.

There is a company called Warren Cutlery that sells a carving set with a handle and various removable blades. These blades can be purchased separately and used for a mini kit.

MULTI-FUNCTION KNIVES

There is a multitude of multi-function knives on the market today. Some are useful for survival and some are not. Others are just plain overkill. If you choose a multi-function knife, use the "KISS" method (Keep It Simple Stupid), as some of these knives try to provide you with everything but the kitchen sink (remember MacGyver?). These knives are hard to handle (some of the handles are thicker than the knife is high) and provide more options than you need.

A good design should provide you with one or two blades and maybe an awl. Most also provide you with a can opener, which is not a bad thing. A long-standing standard is based on the Boy Scout Pocket Knife. It provides a drop-point blade, an awl, a can opener and a bottle opener with screwdriver blade. The military survival folder, which is slightly larger, is based on this design and is used in many military survival kits. The entire knife is made from stainless steel. I keep one of these in each pack in a small pouch as a backup to my main blade.

Victorinox, makers of the Original Swiss Army Knife, makes some decent knives (and also the kitchen sink models) for survival situations. All their knives are high quality and the range of options is staggering. Again, keep it simple. One of my favorites is the "Hunter," which has a good size (3-1/4 inch) locking drop-point blade and an excellent saw. It also has a skinner blade and an awl with an eyehole

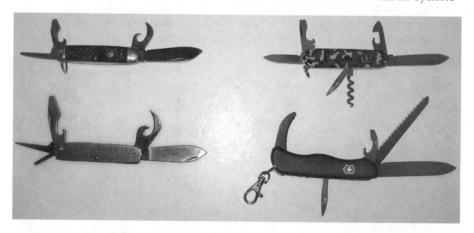

Clockwise from upper left is the Boy Scout Knife, the Victorinox Spartan, the Victorinox Hunter and the military survival folder.

73

The ToolLogic Survival Light/Fire knife is shown here in the closed position with an attached lanyard. The whistle can be seen just below the lanyard hole. Right side of photo shows knife with blade open and flint removed.

in it for sewing. Overall it is 4-3/8 inches long. Of course, it has a can opener/ screwdriver blade, tweezers, toothpick and corkscrew, but the first four blades mentioned are my reason for purchasing the knife. Another Victorinox I like is the "Tinker," which is 3-1/2 inches overall with a 2-3/8-inch main blade. It's nice to throw in small kits as a backup to a main blade.

A new type of multi-function knife has been introduced by ToolLogic. Their three models include the Survival Light, the Survival Light/Water and the Survival Light/Fire, which is the one in which I had the most interest. This knife, although a lock-blade folder, is rather clever. First, it has a 2-3/4-inch sheepfoot blade with serrations at the back (serrations are good for cutting cordage or rope) and a thumbhole for one-hand opening. The Zytel handle has been designed with a survival whistle built into the back end, a lanyard hole and a pocket clip on the side. The top portion of the handle has a compartment that holds a 1-5/8 x 1/4-inch diameter Firesteel flint in a handle with "O"-ring seals (overall length is 3-1/8 inches). The compartment will also hold a standard Mag-Lite Solitaire AAA battery flashlight in place of the flint. The knife blade was also designed with a special notch, just behind the serrated portion of the blade, to use as a striker for the flint, to preserve the knife edge. This is a great little knife for a small kit or as a backup to the main knife in a larger kit. As for being multi-functional, it gives you a knife, a whistle and a fire starter.

Specialty Knives

The following knives do not fit into any other category but are ideal for survival kits.

The Christy Survival Knife, which I have put in many mini survival kits (it fits very nicely in small survival tins), has a history that dates back before WWII and was used during the war in survival kits for pilots and many other armed forces personnel. It is very slim and measures only 3 inches long x 1/2 inch high x 3/16 inch thick. It can be opened (and closed) with one hand and has four locking positions, including closed, so you can slide out only that portion of the blade that you need. The entire blade is safely hidden when in the closed position, as it slides inside the outer frame, which also becomes the knife's handle when opened. Obviously, this is not a large knife, and I would prefer that it be a backup to a main blade. But if you only have a mini kit, a knife is a knife, and this little gem is much better than no knife at all. Completely constructed from stainless steel, it has a small ring on the back. As a survival backup, one of these knives on your key ring may not be a bad idea.

SPECIALTY KNIVES

The Christy knife is shown here in both the closed (top) and open positions (bottom).

This next knife was only recently introduced, but I think it will become a favorite for survival purposes. When I first saw it, I wasn't sure what to think, but I knew I had to have one. It's not a folder, but it is not your normal fixed-blade knife either; it's a revolver (no not a gun). Made by SOG, the knife is called the SEAL-REVOLVER. It is 10 inches overall in length with a 4-3/4-inch stainless-steel clip-point blade with serrations at the rear. However, if you depress a button on the side of the handle, the blade revolves around and a 4-3/4-inch saw rotates out of the handle while the blade goes inside. Because the blade and saw are made from one solid piece of stainless steel, this is actually a fixed-blade knife with a handle that revolves around it.

At first I wasn't sure about the safety aspects of this "thing," but it is well–designed. The handle is made of Zytel, which has stainless-steel liners for both strength and durability. The pin that holds the blade, or saw, in place is substantial and travels well through the hole provided in each. It comes with a Kydex sheath, and the knife can be carried in either the blade-out or saw-out position.

With all knives come warnings, and this knife is no different. Both the knife and saw are extremely sharp and caution must be taken when revolving the blade around. Although I have not cut myself with it, I have read some reviews where it sounds like some reviewers may have. This should be a good all-around

The SOG SEAL-REVOLVER with both blades revealed. Before using the knife one of these blades must be rotated and locked within the handle.

FOLDING KNIVES

FAST FACTS:

Despite its name, stainless steel can still rust if not maintained properly. Some knives are made from other non-steel materials such as cobalt, titanium and ceramic in order to eliminate the rust factor all together.

survival knife for medium and large kits, as it is truly a multi-purpose knife (Have I mentioned that multi-purpose is a good thing?).

FOLDING KNIVES

Although the multi-function knives mentioned earlier are all folding knives, we will now discuss folding knives that have only one, and usually larger, blade. With a larger blade, a folder can be a primary survival knife. A folder is easier to carry and requires less room in a survival kit. Again, if you go this way, buy quality and get a locking blade.

There are innumerable folding knives on the market today. As a main survival knife, you want a substantial one. Again, pick a reputable manufacturer. Some commercially available folders that I have used are the Gerber Gator Knife with 5-inch blade, Gerber E-Z-Out with 3-inch blade, and various models by SOG, Kershaw, Benchmade, Emerson, AL Mar and Browning. Of course, there are many other manufacturers with good folders.

What you need in a survival folder is for the knife to be substantial. It already has a weakness by being a folder, so look for a knife that is well made (you don't want it to rattle when the blade is locked open). Also, don't buy big just to buy big. I once had a young lady in a class who had a folder half her size. I asked her how she chose that knife, and she said a salesperson in a store told her it was just right for her needs. She had difficulty using it. Get a feel for the knife, both open and closed, in your hand. You want it to feel comfortable, not foreign. In a survival situation, you will most likely use this tool more than any other, and you want it to work, yet feel agreeable with your grip.

From left to right, a Gerber 4-1/2-inch clip-point E-Z-Out with serrations, a SOG 4-1/2-inch drop-point Flash II and a Benchmade with a tanto blade, shown as a type of blade NOT to carry for survival.

The author's original Paul knife. A slightly smaller version is now available from Lone Wolf Knives.

Before moving on to fixed-blade knives, this might be a good time to discuss backup blades. Once a main blade is selected, there is nothing wrong, in my opinion, with selecting another smaller supplemental blade. We have already established the importance of a knife in a survival situation, and because I am a person who believes in redundancy, having an extra knife seems only prudent. For this reason, a small pocket folder will always be on your person and can serve as a backup to your main blade. There are many choices for a backup folder, but what I suggest is a knife sized so it can live in your pocket. The following knife is one that could fill that need.

This folder has a different, and very unique, locking mechanism from all others. Called the Paul knife, it is named after Paul W. Poehlmann, the man who designed and patented the axial locking mechanism in the early 1970s. This locking mechanism is unique in that you pinch the button (which is at the swivel point for the blade) between your thumb and forefinger and smoothly snap the handle away from the blade. The mechanism locks the blade in both the open and closed positions, which makes the knife safe for pocket carry. With a little practice, this knife becomes a very handy, one-handed-opening knife. It also features a great full flat-grind drop-point blade.

Unfortunately, the original Paul (which was 3-3/4 inches closed with a 2-1/2-inch blade) was only produced by Gerber Legendary Blades from 1977 to 1986, and then again in 1996 for only two years. Although used knives can occasionally be found, they are rare. Fortunately, a scaled-down version (3-1/8 inches closed with a 2-1/4-inch blade) is now available from Lone Wolf Knives. Only slightly

Shown here are the U.S.A.F. Pilot Survival Knife (top left), the SOG Seal Pup (top right), the Ontario TAC by Randall (bottom left), the TOPS ATC-LOBO (bottom right) and the little TOPS Sparrow Hawke (center).

FIXED-BLADE KNIVES

smaller, it is a great knife for all but the smallest survival kit (or pocket carry) and can be obtained without scales (handles), which make it very thin for packaging. Although small for a main folder, it makes a great supplemental blade and is safe for pocket carry. Whether it is a Paul knife or another small folder, a supplemental backup blade is a good idea in my book (no pun intended).

QUICK TIP:

The best survival knife is the one you have with you. **BE PREPARED!**

FIXED-BLADE KNIVES

For all but the smallest kits, my preference for a survival knife is a fixed-blade knife. I have already indicated that two of my reasons for this are no moving parts and one-piece construction. For these reasons, they are intrinsically stronger. Keep in mind that a primary fixed-blade survival knife does not have to be big, but it does have to be rugged. It should feel comfortable in your hand and have enough blade to perform required chores. Most of my primary survival blades are in the 4-1/2- to 5-inch blade length. They are high quality, built for abuse (not that you want to abuse a knife) and have a comfortable handle that does not get slippery when wet. These are all important features.

A knife that was built for survival – and is still issued – is the Air Force Pilot Survival Knife. Manufactured by Camillus of high-carbon steel with a 5-inch blade, this was my first survival knife (about 30 years ago) and remained so for quite some time. It has a sawtooth back (which works marginally) and a considerable pummel (butt) for hammering. My only aversion is that it is still sold with a leather sheath. It does have a pocket on the sheath with a sharpening stone, and it is sold at the very reasonable price of about $35 from suppliers such as Brigade Quartermasters.

Another fixed-blade knife that is good for survival is the U.S.M.C. Ka-Bar. This knife is also manufactured by Camillus of high-carbon steel; however, the blade length is 7 inches. This knife has been around since 1942 and was designed for the U.S. Marines fighting in WWII. It is still a formidable survival knife if you want

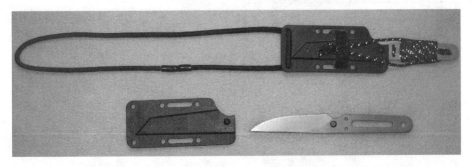

The author's small fixed-blade neck knife is shown in its sheath, with reflective cord wrapped around the handle. Note small lanyard for knife butt is held up on the sheath with Velcro so it cannot get snagged. On bottom is the same knife as it comes from the factory without the cord wrap on the skeletonized handles.

FIXED-BLADE KNIVES

a longer blade. Now also available in a shorter blade length of 5-1/4 inches, both versions are available at a cost of about $65 from the same suppliers who sell the U.S.A.F. Pilot Survival Knife.

A new line of knives specifically designed for survival by Jeff Randall are currently being manufactured by the well-respected Ontario Knife Company. The first knife, called the TAK, has a zinc-phosphate-finished carbon-steel drop-point blade with a full flat grind. Blade thickness is 3/16 inch at the back and overall length is 10 inches with a blade length of 4-1/2 inches. It has canvass Micarta ergonomic handle slabs, which are attached with stainless steel screws, for increased grip when wet. The pommel has been extended and has a lanyard hole. Cost is about $70.00. Because of the full flat grind, it is especially adept at cutting and carving wood, which is what I need it to do. I carry this knife as my main blade when I am not carrying my "leg-rig," which will be discussed under the next section. My only displeasure with the knife is the sheath, which does not ride well on my waist. I have, therefore, replaced the original sheath with a BlackHawk Airborne Deluxe Knife Sheath, with Kydex insert, as I always carry my main knife in the field in a dropped-down leg rig (which is my preference). This sheath also provides space for my multi-tool.

It should be noted that Ontario Knife Company has very recently introduced the RAT-7, which is also designed by Jeff Randall. It is a larger version of the TAK, being 12 inches overall with a 6.5-inch blade. I haven't played with this new model yet, but it is my understanding that it is offered with a new Cordura sheath with a gear pocket and Kydex blade insert being made by SpecOps Brand.

Another knife that will satisfy survival needs is the SOG Seal Pup. It is stainless steel with a powder-coated 4-3/4-inch blade with a 1-inch serrated section at the back. At a cost of about $65, it has Zytel handles with a lanyard hole. SOG has also recently introduced the SOG Field Pup and Field Knife, which appear to be two additional knives suitable for survival.

A company that produces several handcrafted knives that would fill survival needs is TOPS (Tactical OPS USA). One of their knives I have tried is the ATC-LOBO. This carbon-steel knife is 10-1/4 inches overall with a 5-1/4-inch blade. It has linen Micarta handles and a Kydex and Cordura LBE sheath, with a pouch. When I purchased the knife, I asked that the pouch be made slightly larger to accommodate my multi-tool and a 4-inch flint. They supplied the knife with the modified pouch (at no extra cost) for $180.00. This knife is extremely sturdy, but I prefer a full flat-grind blade, and this blade is ground more like the U.S.A.F. Pilot Survival Knife (not a bad thing, just a difference in preference).

One fixed-blade knife that I bought from TOPS, which I carry every day as a supplement blade (whether in field attire or a suit), is called the Sparrow Hawke. It is made from carbon steel and is only 5 inches long with a 2-inch full flat-grind blade. It comes with a small Kydex belt sheath, and it is the best little

DID YOU KNOW?

The Bowie Knife was designed by Rezin Bowie. It was made famous, however, by his brother James, who died in battle at the Alamo.

FIXED-BLADE KNIVES

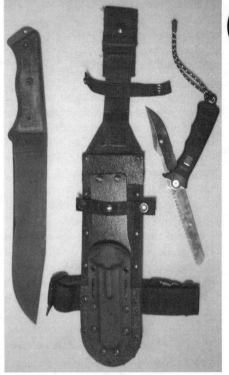

The author's piggyback knife rig is capable of carrying a large fixed-blade knife like the Ontario RTAK and a medium survival knife such as the SOG SEAL Revolver. (Photo by Janice McCann.)

knife for whittling and other small carving needs (like making a spoon in the field). Although not large enough for a main blade, it is great for small survival chores.

Before moving on to large fixed-blade knives, it should be mentioned that a smaller fixed-blade knife can also be carried as a supplemental knife for survival purposes. There are various models of small fixed-blade knives, many of which have very thin, or skeletonized, handles. I don't prefer skeletonized handles as a norm, but they have their place.

Whenever I go into the field, I always carry a small fixed-blade knife on a neck lanyard as a backup. This knife, the MDF (for modified drop-point) Stiff K.I.S.S., is manufactured by Columbia River Knife & Tool Company (CRKT). It is 7-1/4 inches overall with a 3-1/2-inch blade and skeletonized handle. Designed by Ed Halligan, it is made from stainless steel with a bead-blast finish. The reason I chose this knife is because it had a skeletonized handle. I wanted a small fixed-blade backup with a handle that I could wrap with enough cord to tie the knife to a stick for a spear (this is why it is a backup, as you would never risk losing your main blade by using it for a spear). Because of the skeletonized handle and its available holes and slot, it was perfect for wrapping with cord. It comes in a black Zytel sheath, which includes a belt clip, screws and lanyard for a variety of carry options. One of my survival buddies has one mounted upside down on the shoulder strap of his pack.

I should mention a safety matter involving neck lanyards, as I see many people carrying everything from knives to compasses on a neck lanyard. If you wear a neck lanyard, make sure it has a break-away. This can be a section that was cut and sewn back together with only several stitches or, in the case of mine, a rubber tube that holds the lanyard together. You want the neck lanyard to securely hold your gear, but not so strong that it won't break in an emergency. If you ever climb down an embankment and slip, and your neck lanyard gets hung up on a branch or other immobile object, and you keep going, you could be choked to death.

There are various other knives available with thin or skeletonized handles that will serve this purpose. They would include such knives as Columbia's Shoshone Fixed Blade, a 6-inch knife with a 3-7/8-inch blade, or the Chimney Rock Fixed Blade, an 8-3/8-inch knife with a 4-inch blade. Both come with a nylon sheath that can be neck worn. Two other manufacturers that offer knives such as these are Boker and Camillus (with a nice model called the C.U.D.A. Arclite Neck Knife). Keep in mind these are backups, not a main blade, except for small kits.

The fixed-blade knives described above are by no means the only ones adequate, or useful, as survival knives. These are knives with which I am familiar and that have served my purposes in survival. There are plenty of others that I have not purchased or tested but that would be more than useful in a survival situation. It is up to you to handle, try and experiment with a knife that YOU will depend on in a survival situation.

LARGE FIXED-BLADE KNIVES OR MACHETES

For certain environments, or for large survival kits such as vehicle or aircraft kits, you may want a large fixed-blade knife or a machete. This might be especially true in a jungle environment, where a machete is more a necessity than an option. When I'm out on a 10-day advanced survival course in the Adirondack Mountains, I will often carry a larger fixed-blade knife in combination with a medium-sized blade. The larger blade is ideal for brush removal, chopping and splitting wood, and various other chores that are too demanding for a smaller knife. I prefer to carry these two blades piggyback on a leg sheath I have built for this purpose (see photo on previous page).

Becker Knife & Tool (now owned by Camillus) is one manufacturer that specializes in various large fixed-blade knives and machetes, all of which have been designed by the survival knife expert, Ethan Becker. They all have the same handle, which is made from an extremely tough glass-filled nylon that provides a good comfortable grip. Various models are offered, only some of which will be discussed here.

The first two are called the Becker Combat Utility Bowies, which come in 7- and 9-inch models. I have used both and have settled on the 9-inch model, as it provides the greater cutting ability. These bowies, which have extremely sharp flat-ground clip-point blades, are made of carbon steel and are built for hard use. The blades are black-matte epoxy powder coated for protection from the elements. Both come with a nylon, jump-safe sheath with a Kydex insert and utility pouch (which just happens to be the perfect size to hold an Altoids-tin survival kit). Cost is about $50 and $60, respectfully.

The other Becker blade, which is great for jungle or heavily wooded areas, is the Patrol Machete, a powerful chopper with a bolo-style blade that is forward weighted. It measures 19 inches overall, has a 14-inch blade (of carbon steel) and weighs 19 ounces. This machete also serves well as a drawknife for when you need to make a bow in the field. Its size allows it to be carried on a pack as well as in a

From top to bottom are the Becker BK-9 Combat/Utility Knife with 9-inch blade, Ontario RTAK Survival/Bush Knife with 10-inch blade, Becker Patrol Machete with 14-inch blade and a military 18-inch blade machete.

boat, aircraft, vehicle or ATV kit. Provided with a black ballistic cloth sheath lined with plastic multiple tie-down grommets, it costs about $75.

Another good large fixed-blade knife is the Ontario RTAK (Randall's Training & Adventure Knife). It was specifically designed as a survival/bush knife by the professional survival training team at Randall's Adventure and Training (RAT). This is the same team that designed the TAK and RAT-7, discussed at length under the fixed-blade knife section above.

The blade of the RTAK, designed for wilderness survival and jungle environments, is the perfect cross between a large sheath knife and a machete. It is 17-1/8 inches long with a 10-inch full flat-grind, clip-point blade. The handle has been offset 5 degrees from the blade to increase chopping power. It has an extended pommel with a lanyard hole and linen Micarta handles. The ambidextrous black nylon sheath has a gear pocket, lashing holes and a leg lanyard. Although large, I would prefer a Kydex sheath or a sheath with a Kydex insert. If you need a multi-purpose knife/machete for a large kit (especially vehicle kits) or personal carry, this may be the one. Cost is about $80.

The last large fixed-blade is the military 18-inch machete. The longest of the blades discussed here, it is manufactured with heavy zinc-phosphate-parkerized carbon steel. Durable plastic handles are riveted to the steel tang, and it has a lanyard hole. This is a well-balanced machete and will perform well for a price of about $20. If you make a kit for a jungle environment, or want to keep a real chopper in your vehicle, this will do the job. Just keep in mind that a machete is a supplemental blade. It is great for clearing brush and trails, and chopping, but don't expect to clean a fish or do fine whittling.

If you choose to carry a large fixed-blade knife, do so for its required ability to accomplish specific tasks, or as an addition to your main blade. Don't do it for macho reasons, such as looking like Rambo. Survival is not the movies, and it's not a game, so you need to carry equipment that is practical.

Knife Design	Intended Uses
Folder or Pocket knife	For everyday urban use or light field work. The blade can be hidden within the handle
Hunting or Bowie	For light to heavy field work. Can be used for digging ground. Usually fixed blade. Other variations include survival knives with other components stored within the sheath.
Military or Tactical	Occupational or military use. Improved metallurgical properties (tensile strength) in the blade. Usually low or no luster finish. Some models have a self-sharpening sheath.
Vintage or Collector	These knives are not usually used in any field work to preserve their values and condition. Vintage knives are usually functional. Some collector knives have a dull edge usually for display and can be functional to some extent. Some include commemorative impressions on the blade, handle or sheath.

MULTI-PURPOSE TOOLS

Before the Leatherman Tool was invented less than 20 years ago, there were no "multi-purpose" tools, per se. Now there is a staggering collection of multi-tools being offered by many manufacturers, such as Leatherman, Gerber, SOG, Buck, Kershaw, etc. I believe that these tools have a definite place in survival. Larger and more durable than multi-purpose knives, they almost all have a good set of pliers, which definitely come in handy for various survival tasks. On one survival course, a lady student kept asking to use my "pot picker-upper" as she

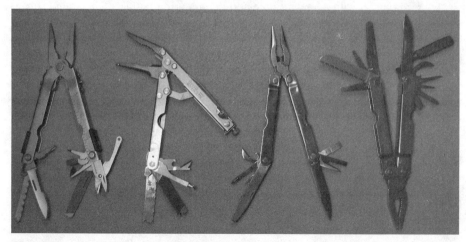

From left to right are the Gerber Multi-Purpose Tool (the author's preferred tool), a Kershaw locking-pliers tool, an Original Leatherman tool and SOG Power Pliers.

pointed to my multi-purpose tool. She liked to use them to lift her hot pot out of the coals of a fire. However, I have used the pliers for various chores, from holding a slippery fish while it was scaled, to bending wire to make a fish net out of a head net.

There are so many of these type tools to choose from that I will only state you should decide what components you desire and then find a quality unit that provides them. Some components that I desire are pliers, a saw and scissors. All have at least one knife blade, so that's a given as a backup blade.

I have experimented with numerous makes and models, and I keep going back to the Gerber, as they open with one hand. This is an advantage if one hand is already occupied, or injured, when you need to use it. The one I carry has pliers and cutters, a saw (which can be easily replaced with any saber-saw blade), a pair of Fiskars scissors, a partially serrated blade, a can opener and several different screwdriver blades. I modified the smallest screwdriver blade, grinding it into a useable awl.

Before leaving multi-purpose tools, it should be mentioned there is a new breed of smaller tools, some of which can also be useful for survival. One of these is the Leatherman Micra, which is a small pair of folding scissors that is also a multi-purpose tool. It includes a small – but very sharp – knife blade, medium and small screwdriver blades, a small file, tweezers and a can opener. The scissors have 1-inch jaws and work well. For a small kit or your key ring, this little tool can be a great addition.

The bottom line is if you choose to make a multi-purpose tool a part of your survival kit, be realistic and select one that works for you.

HACKSAW BLADE

By hacksaw blade, I don't mean a complete hacksaw blade. Hacksaw blades can be cut down so they can be carried as a small-duty saw in a mini survival kit. They can also be used as a flint striker by using the back side (without the teeth). You can cut (or break) off a length that will fit your kit, and if your kit has enough space, you can wrap one end with tape to protect your hand when sawing. I have also ground the teeth off one end for a handhold. They are very flat and store in a very small space. I wanted to protect myself from the teeth on the one I carry on my survival key ring, so I filed a slot, or groove, in a small

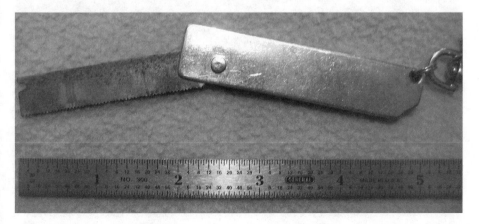

The short folding hacksaw-blade carrier made by the author.

piece of aluminum, 5/32-inch thick and 3 inches long, with a hacksaw blade. I then drilled a hole through one end and used a rivet in a short piece of hacksaw as a pivot. The blade can be stored with teeth faced in, in the holder, or pivoted out for use. I now always have a small saw in my pocket.

WIRE SURVIVAL SAWS

One of the most useful survival saws for its size is the wire survival saw because it is small enough to be carried in almost any sized kit. Two types are available, with the first being supplied in all U.S. military survival kits. Basically a 16-inch wire made from rust-resistant high-tensile-strength steel, it is specially coated so the result provides aggressive multi-directional cutting teeth. When not in use, it rolls up into a small space for storage. Unroll it when you need it, and you have a saw.

To use this saw, split rings are placed on both ends in the holes provided. You then place your first two fingers in each ring and pull the wire saw back and forth, with minimal pressure, over the item you want to cut. For easier sawing, you can place a short piece of small stick or branch through the split rings, which provides a complete handhold at each end. This saw will cut wood, bone, plastic, soft metals and ice. Manufactured by Mouli Manufacturing Corp., it is available from Ranger Joe's.

For one-handed use, cut a thick branch, about 3/4 inch in diameter and 4 to 6 inches longer than the saw. Make a groove in each end of the branch. Place one of the split rings in the groove on one end. Then, by gently bending the branch, place the other split ring in the groove on the other end. Use minimal pressure when using the saw in this manner.

Made in England, the second type of survival wire saw is available, as far as I know, only from Brigade Quartermasters. It is made from eight woven stainless-steel metal strands that form a 28-inch sawing edge. Although I personally feel that the U.S. military wire saw cuts more aggressively, I carry this saw in many of my mini kits, such as my Altoids-tin kit, because it rolls up a lot smaller and tighter than the military one. Again, I use different items for different kits, depending on size and configuration. Another nice feature of this saw is that it will slide over itself without getting snagged, which allows you to

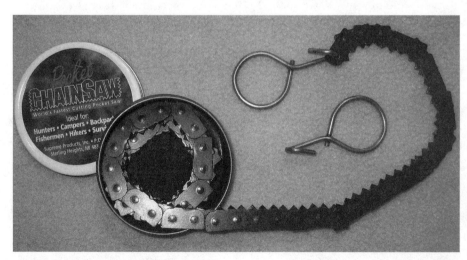

The Pocket ChainSaw, which comes in a can.

WIRE SURVIVAL SAWS

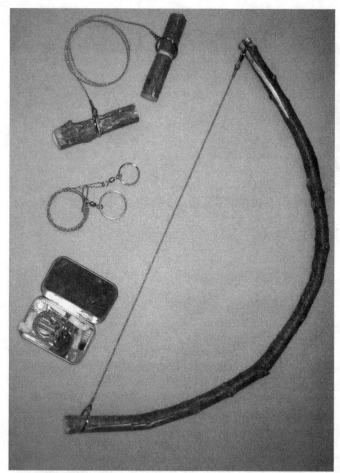

The survival wire saw can be made into a bow saw or used with short branch pieces for handholds. The saw, made in England, is also shown rolled up small enough for storage in an Altoids-tin kit.

The technique for using the wire survival saw, with handholds, for cutting a branch (right). A bow saw, made from a branch and a survival wire saw, can be used for cutting larger pieces of wood (above). (Photos by Janice McCann.)

The Gerber folding saw in both open and closed positions.

use the saw as a snare (multi-use item). The saw is used in the same manner as the military saw.

POCKET CHAIN SAWS

This is another survival saw that rolls up and is stored in a can, 1 inch high by 2-3/4 inches in diameter. It is called the Pocket ChainSaw and is manufactured by Supreme Products and offered by Ranger Joe's. It's made from high-strength, heat-treated steel, and is 28 inches long. It has 124 bi-directional teeth that really cut fast. It is used with finger rings, like the wire survival saw, but you must keep the blade straight for it to work properly. Because it is housed in a small can, it can be carried in a small kit or your pocket, or stored in your vehicle. This is a clever device for some serious survival cutting.

SMALL FOLDING SAWS

A small folding saw, often called a pruning saw, is a good addition to a larger survival kit. These types of saws are available from many camp stores and fold within their own handle. A very small and light one that I carry was originally made by Gerber but is now made by Bear MGC. It is 6-3/4 inches long by 1-7/8 inches wide by 9/16 inch deep. Weighing only 3-1/2 ounces, it has a very aggressive cutting blade and cuts on the pull stroke. One lives in my truck and one lives in my pack.

LARGE FOLDING SAWS

Although large folding saws cannot be used in smaller kits, they definitely have their place in larger kits and vehicle kits. I normally carry one when canoe camping, as they make cutting firewood much less of a chore. They are also handy in a vehicle kit when a small tree falls across the road and you have to move it in order to pass. They are available in various configurations, but I will discuss two that are particularly suitable for survival use.

The Sven-Saw, which is a triangular-type saw with a 15-inch blade when assembled, is well-known and available at most camp stores. When collapsed, the saw blade rotates into the top of the frame and the frame slides into the handle, which makes a storage-size package of 17-1/2 inches long by 1-1/2

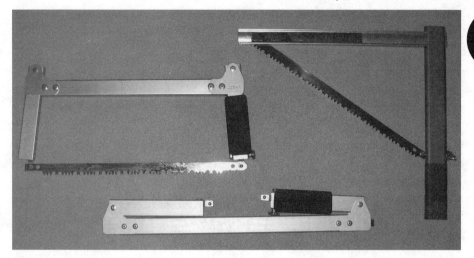

On the left is the Sawvivor, shown open and then folded. On the right is the Sven-Saw in the assembled position.

inches wide by 1/2 inch thick. The frame is made from aluminum and the blade is Swedish steel. My only criticism with this saw is that when you are sawing a good size log, and you start getting halfway through, you start to lose a full stroke with the saw because ends of the saw start hitting the wood. This is due to its triangular shape.

The second saw is the Sawvivor Folding Saw. Because of its configuration, there isn't a problem with a shortened stroke when sawing through a small log. This saw is super light and is offered in two blade sizes, 15 and 18 inches. With a strong anodized-aluminum frame that folds to a compact size for easy carrying and storage, this saw has no loose hardware, so there is nothing to lose. The handle is padded and the saw blade stores inside the frame when not in use. The small version weighs only 9.7 ounces and the larger version 11.5 ounces. I have carried the smaller version strapped to the side of my pack during some outdoor adventures.

SMALL FOLDING TROWELS

It is difficult to carry an actual shovel in a small survival kit, but a small trowel can be used for some digging chores, such as digging a cat hole, digging up the roots of edible plants or moving coals from a fire. Most of the small trowels available at camping stores are made from plastic and the handle does not fold to

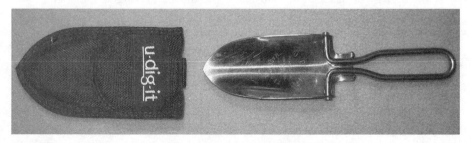

A view of the U-Dig-It trowel in the open position, with its belt pouch at left.

SMALL FOLDING TROWELS

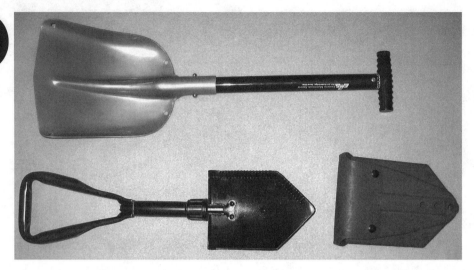

The top shovel is an EMS collapsible shovel, which is ideal for snow. The bottom shovel is the U.S. military folding model with its carrier to the right.

reduce their size. They are light, but you don't want to get them next to a flame; and because they are plastic, they are breakable.

However, there is a small folding trowel made from solid stainless steel. Called the U-Dig-It, it measures only 5-3/4 inches long when folded by 2-1/2 inches wide. The actual trowel, a heavy-duty well-built unit, is 4-1/2 inches long. The handle locks open when in use and is rugged enough to chop roots on plants. When closed, it stores in a supplied ballistic nylon belt pouch, which can be carried on your belt when in the field or packed easily in a small kit.

FOLDING SHOVELS

A folding or collapsible shovel is a necessary item for most vehicle survival kits. It can be a digging shovel, with a sharp point for desert and wilderness country, or a flat model for snow country. This type of shovel is also recommended for packs and snowmobile kits when adventuring in snow country.

The most durable folding shovel I have used is the U.S. military folding shovel. When in the U.S. Marine Corps, we called these an E-Tool (for entrenching tool). It has a sharp front and side edge for digging and chopping, and it folds down and stores in a carrier for storage.

There are various models of collapsible snow shovels available at mountain-climbing shops and at various camp stores such as EMS.

If you are building a large kit, include a shovel. It will quickly pay for itself when in a situation where only a shovel can produce the desired effect. I always carry the military folder in my truck, year round, and the EMS collapsible shovel in the winter.

CHAPTER 8

MEDICAL

First and foremost, this book is about survival kits. I have stated that I don't propose to instruct the reader on survival skills, nor do I now intend to provide medical or first-aid advice. The purpose of this chapter is to identify certain components that could be useful for medical treatment in a survival situation and how to package those components for a survival kit. All of these items may or may not work for you, and you might even decide to select items not discussed. Like knives, there are basics, but you must ultimately decide what components work for you and which ones will fit in the space you allocate.

If you are not well versed in first aid, I would suggest that you attend a course, such as the Red Cross Wilderness First Aid Course, so that you have the basics for treatment should an emergency situation arise. It's not a good time to learn when the blood is flowing.

PRIORITY

In regard to medical supplies, I try to carry components that will allow me to treat wounds and manage infection. For me, these are the basics, and for a mini kit, it is all I can include. Of course, as a first-aid kit grows in size, the diversity and quantity of items can increase.

SELECTING COMPONENTS

Wound Management

The idea here is to carry items that will allow you to deal with a wound. At the very least, I carry some wound closure strips such as butterfly bandages or Steri-Strips (illegal in some areas), depending on the configuration of my kit. I also carry, at the minimum, a triple antibacterial ointment such as Neosporin to manage infection and some alcohol prep pads to clean the wound. Keep in mind that alcohol prep pads are a multi-use item, as they also work nicely as fire starters.

As a kit grows in size, I add items that will allow me to stop bleeding, which is always a priority. One of these items is trauma pads for soaking up blood. As a note, sanitary napkins are ideal to carry and use as trauma pads. They are sterile and much cheaper than commercial trauma pads. I also carry the military field dressings, as they were made for this purpose. It is a good idea to carry non-adherent sterile pads to place over the wound before wrapping it up, and some sterile dressing for wrapping it.

In large kits, for heavy bleeding, you can also carry blood-clot powder. The only type previously available commercially was from veterinarian supply houses. However, there is now a product called Quik-Clot, which is a granulated mineral substance that you pour on a bleeding wound. At a price of about $20.00, it works by soaking up the blood and gets clotting agents concentrated on the surface of the wound. For more information, check www.z-medica.com.

In larger kits, I carry both strip and knuckle bandages (I always seem to need the knuckle bandages for some reason) in addition to Povidone Iodine Swabs (to clean wounds), Tincture of Benzoin (which can protect skin and be used as an adhesive), larger packages of antibacterial ointment and an irrigation syringe for cleaning wounds.

If you are with other people and the kit is not just for yourself, you may want to carry nitrate examination gloves, a CPR mask and an infectious control bag to help control infections.

For all but mini kits, you might think about carrying a first-aid pamphlet or booklet to remind you how to handle specific situations.

Medications

I don't like taking a lot of medicine, but a minimal amount can be useful in emergencies. The first on my list is non-prescription painkillers like simple aspirin. Especially for those getting on in years, like myself, aspirin might be a big help if you feel a heart attack coming on, or for simple aches. I also carry Advil (an ibuprofen) for pain because it works for me; some of my buddies prefer Tylenol. The point here is to carry something for pain and to carry what works for you.

The next thing I carry is an antihistamine such as Benadryl for allergies or itching from insect bites. A cream is good for topical treatment of such things as bites, but for allergies a tablet is better. Keep in mind that some tablets can make you drowsy; in a survival situation, you may want to live with the itch.

An anti-diarrheal, such as Imodium AD, might be another choice for a kit. In the event you drink some bad water (which you shouldn't) or your lower tract disagrees with some survival food, diarrhea can quickly cause dehydration, another thing you don't want in a survival situation.

Lastly, if you are allergic to bee stings, you may want to carry an epinephrine. EpiPen, a self-injected epinephrine, can only be obtained with a prescription, so if you think you need to carry some, get with your doctor for a prescription before heading out.

Miscellaneous Items

The following are some miscellaneous items you may want to include as your first-aid kit becomes larger. If you are in an area where Lyme disease is prevalent, a set of tick tweezers is small and easy to carry.

Another item that is useful if you are around snakes, scorpions or nasty bees is a Sawyer Extractor kit. This little kit provides a small vacuum pump and is the only device recommended for removing the venom of snake and scorpion bites and bee stings. Although it comes in a nice little yellow plastic box, it can be removed so it will store in a smaller kit.

If you need a splint in an emergency situation, you can always make one from a tree branch, tent pole, etc. But if a larger kit provides the room, a SAM Splint is made for just this purpose. I even carry one in my medium-size first-aid kit. Made from malleable aluminum, it is foam padded. They can be molded to any body part and are not affected by extremes of temperature. Only 9-1/4 inches long x 4-1/4 inches wide x 3/4 inch thick while folded in the package, they fold out to 36 inches long and weigh only 4 ounces.

Some smaller items you might consider carrying are an Ace bandage, an irrigation syringe, a thermometer, EMT shears, and some safety pins and duct tape (more on duct tape in the next chapter).

One other item not mentioned very often is an emergency dental kit. They are available in many drug stores and can save the day when a tooth problem occurs.

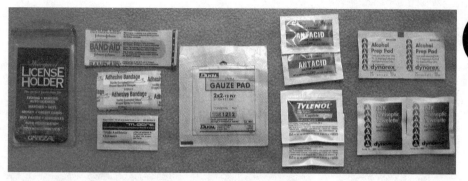

A look at the waterproof pouch and contents for the pocketsize first-aid kit made by the author.

The one I carry is made by DenTek and measures only 3-5/8 inches x 2-5/8 inches x 7/8 inch. It cost only several dollars.

Packaging the Kit

This can range from placing various items within a survival kit to having a separate container for your first-aid equipment. I sometimes use commercially available bags and strip them of the items and start over with my own selection.

On other occasions, I will find a bag that accommodates what I want to pack. It should be noted that anything that can be ruined when wet should be packaged in zip-lock bags or other waterproof containers. For some larger kits, I double-bag the entire kit in large freezer zip-lock bags.

If you are making a kit for water-borne operations, give some thought to a hard waterproof case. Some first-aid kits come in hard waterproof containers but don't necessarily contain your choice of contents. If the container works for your needs, strip it and start over with your selection of needed items. Some small waterproof containers such as the "Otter Box" are available from water sports shops or Campmor. Available in various sizes and configurations, they come in yellow, black and clear, which are nice, as you can see the contents.

MINI TO SMALL FIRST-AID KITS

As indicated above, some small first-aid items can be packaged directly into a mini kit. In many of my mini kits, I place several butterfly bandages, a small package of triple antibiotic ointment, and one or two mini alcohol prep pads. These items cover my requirement to be able to treat wounds and manage infection.

In the small first-aid kit the author carries in his survival pack, individual types of items are packaged in various zip-lock bags to protect them from getting wet.

Build the Perfect Survival Kit

I also make a pocketsize first-aid kit for my students in a small waterproof license holder pouch that measures only 4-1/2 inches long x 2-3/4 inches wide. Although extremely small, it contains the basics: two adhesive Bandages, two butterfly closures, one 2-inch x 2-inch sterile gauze pad, one package of triple antibiotic ointment, four Extra Strength Tylenol, two antacid tablets, two antiseptic towelettes and two alcohol prep pads.

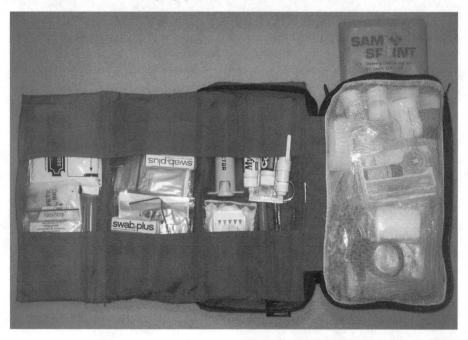

The author's large first-aid kit with three fold-out pallets on left. Note SAM Splint at top right.

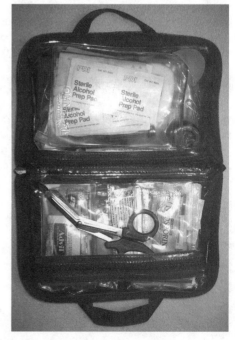

The author's medium-size first-aid kit used during group outings.

Most of my small first-aid kits are packaged in various pouches about 7 inches x 4 inches. I get one of these pouches from EMS and then strip it. It is red on one side and says "First Aid", with clear plastic on the other side and a zipper across the top. I put most of my contents in several of the small waterproof license holders discussed above (or small zip-lock bags) and store them in the larger pouch. I put bandages in one pouch, medicine in another, etc. This allows me to extract only the pouch with the items I need, which is especially useful when it is raining. I include various other items that I prefer, and this is the kit I keep in my survival pack. It is very compact and yet provides the essentials for first aid.

MEDIUM TO LARGE FIRST-AID KITS

For personal carry, a small kit should suffice for most needs. I carry a medium-size kit when out with a small group, and if with students on an advanced survival course, I carry a large kit. The kit size really depends on if you are caring for just yourself or if you are responsible for other people.

My medium kit is built on the same idea as my small kit. Individual item groups are packaged together in waterproof pouches or small zip-lock bags – just more stuff in a bigger pouch. Again, I used a pre-existing red first-aid pouch from EMS (actually made by Adventure Medical Kits), which is about 9 inches wide x 5-1/2 inches high x 2-1/2 inches thick when zipped closed. When un-zipped, it opens to two clear plastic compartments, one on each side, with a zipper across the top section of each. It has carry handles at the top when closed. This makes a nice medium-sized kit, because when you open it, you can see what items are on what side.

For a large kit, I started with a zipped pouch made by OR (Outdoor Research), which manufactures various sized pouches they call Outdoor Organizers. Available in various sizes, they just look like a small pouch when zipped closed. When you unzip them, they have a zippered net-covered section on one side. This is where it gets interesting. The other side unfolds, providing three individual pallet-type sections. Each pallet has differently sized spaces sewn in to accommodate various items. I use the medium-size pouch (11 inches x 6 inches x 2 inches closed) for my large first-aid kit.

COMMERCIAL KITS

I don't usually discuss commercial kits, as this book is about making your own personalized kits. However, if you don't think you have the medical knowledge to select the required items for a survival medical kit, there is a very reputable company that specializes in adventure medical kits. Not so coincidentally, the name of the company is Adventure Medical Kits. The director and founder of this company is Dr. Eric Weiss, who is considered the leading authority on modern wilderness and outdoor medicine. His innovations in wilderness medical kits have continued to raise the standards for outdoor first-aid kits.

Adventure Medical Kits offers first-aid kits in every size and shape. They are broken down into categories such as the Mountain Series, which offers kits with names like Comprehensive, Backcountry, Fundamentals, Daytripper, etc. If you really don't think you can, or want to, make your own medical kit, you can check these kits out in stores such as EMS and Campmor.

ALUMINUM FOIL / SNARE WIRE

CHAPTER 9

MULTI-PURPOSE COMPONENTS

Multi-purpose components are exactly that: items that can be used for more than one purpose. This is an area where you are limited only by your imagination. You want to think outside of the box and innovation is the name of the game.

We have already discussed various components that can be used for multiple uses in the preceding chapters. However, let's go further and examine some of the components that offer us diverse options in their usage.

ALUMINUM FOIL

Aluminum foil is an item that can fit in any size kit, no matter how small. Only the amount that can be carried differs. However, you want to carry as much as possible, and I recommend carrying heavy-duty aluminum foil, as it is much more durable than the normal thin stuff.

As you saw in Chapter 5, aluminum foil can be used to make a cup or small pot to boil water for purification or cooking. You can also wrap the foil around a "Y" stick to make a small frying pan. To cook a fish, just roll it up in the foil and place it in the coals of your fire. It works well as a reflector for cooking and can also be used for signaling (one side is very reflective) or for making fishing lures.

SNARE WIRE

As you will also recall from Chapter 5, we discussed snare wire. My recommendation is to carry at least 10 to 20 feet of 24-gauge wire, which can also be used for various in-field projects and repairs. To make a fishing pole, you can use snare wire to make eyelets on the pole at various points. Wrap the wire around the pole, then make a small loop to be left hanging under the pole, then a couple of more wraps around the pole. You can now run your fishing line down through the loops like on a real fishing pole.

This wire can be used for all kinds of repairs. If you have a boot with the sole flapping or falling off, wrap the wire around the boot to hold the sole on (then wrap it with duct tape – see next heading). Use the wire to repair broken glasses or replace the hinge pin on glasses. In a pinch, it can even be used to lash items together. The uses are only limited by your creativity.

I have carried snare wire by wrapping it around a small sewing bobbin so it doesn't get kinked. Unroll the amount you need and leave the rest on the bobbin.

DUCT TAPE

Duct tape is the magical sticking device of all adventurers and survivors and is another item that can be used for repairs and for constructing various in-field projects. It can be used to tape together most broken items, such as canoes, oars, boats, tent poles, etc. It will also repair most rips in clothing, packs, bags, tents, tarps, rain gear and, as indicated earlier, boot soles. If you don't have moleskin or Molefoam, use it to cover a blister. Most loggers carry strips of it inside their jacket

DUCT TAPE

in the event they cut themselves with a chainsaw. They just duct-tape the gaping wound closed until they can get to medical help. As with most multi-purpose items, duct tape provides an opportunity for your innovativeness to transcend.

There are many manufacturers of duct tape, but you should buy only the best. In the October 2000 issue, *Backpacker Magazine* did a test on duct tape. Their testing indicated that Manco, Anchor and 3M Scotch A/C Ventilating Duct Tape produced the best all-round results. I normally carry 3M Scotch brand, but I also carry the military 90 M.P.H. tape in olive drab (available from military suppliers). This stuff has allegedly been used to temporarily repair shot-up military planes so they could get back to base. Only the government knows for sure, but I find it works well for me.

Whatever brand you select, you will find the problem is it comes on a large 3-inch cardboard spool with an outside diameter of about 6 inches. This obviously won't do for our purposes (except possibly for a vehicle kit). Therefore, we have to re-roll it so it will fit in our kits. Many camp books recommend that you roll some on your water bottle or on a pencil. This certainly works, but sometimes we need it even smaller for our mini kits. I re-roll duct tape in a configuration that allows it to fit where I want it.

For mini kits, such as tins, I use flat pieces, which I place on the backing material that labels come on (use the shiny side and the tape will peel right off when you need it). When I use all the labels on an 8-1/2 x 11-inch sheet, I save that backing material and put it in a file folder for later use. You can make individual pieces that fit in the bottom of the tin, or cut a piece twice the length and fold it in half after you cover it with the duct tape. This provides a very thin package, and although not a lot of tape, it provides you with something.

Another thing I do for small kits, if I want it flat, is use a piece of thin plastic 2 inches high x 3/4 inch wide. I then re-roll the duct tape on the plastic. It provides rounded corners, but still provides a low profile. For some configurations, I re-roll the tape on a small plastic tube or 2–inch-long dowel. The tape can then be re-rolled to the diameter that will fit in your kit. The larger the diameter, the more tape you get to carry. For larger kits, I use the same tube or dowel method. You will be amazed at how much tape you can get in a small-diameter package.

For a repair kit, I will sometimes wrap a small amount of duct tape around a small plastic tube that has a screw-on cover. You then can store needles, etc., inside

From left to right, a new roll of duct tape, re-rolled on a flat piece of plastic, re-rolled on a small plastic dowel, rolled around a plastic tube with screw lid and on pieces of label backing material.

the tube. I could go on, but I'm sure you've got the idea. You need duct tape in your kit; you just need to make the package smaller.

LARGE GARBAGE BAGS

I recommend carrying two to three contractor-grade garbage/leaf bags in any kit they will fit in. I use the Husky Contractor Clean-Up Bags, as they are 3 millimeters thick, or 1 millimeter thicker than most others, which are 2 millimeters or less. You can also use 55-gallon drum liners, which are larger, but I find they take up more room in a kit and are usually of the 2-millimeter thickness. For a large kit they should be fine. These bags can be used for rain protection, shelter, bedding, insulation, water collection or any other idea you can come up with.

For rain protection, you can do one of two things. If you have a rain hat, you can simply cut a hole for your head in the bottom of the bag and pull the bag over your body. If you are simply waiting out the rain, don't cut holes for your arms. This will keep most of your body dry until the rain stops. If you need to be active, cut holes for your arms.

If you don't have a hat, then cut a hole for your face just below one bottom corner. Again, place the bag over your body and use the corner to cover your head,

A contractor clean-up bag can be used as rain gear when you have a brimmed hat (as on the left), when you don't or, as in photo, when you only have a visor cap. In either configuration, holes can be cut for the arms if activity is necessary. (Photos by Janice McCann.)

sort of like a poncho. Also, if you have a ball cap or other type visor, you can use it to protrude through the face opening to divert water from your face.

For use as shelter, you can cut open the bottom of two bags. String your parachute cord through both and attach to two trees or other appropriate uprights. Duct tape the two bags together, end-to-end, and you have a makeshift tube tent. Be sure to keep both ends open so you don't suffocate.

You can also cut the side seems on a bag, or two, and use them as a tarp-like shelter to provide protection from the rain or the sun.

If you want soft bedding to sleep on, fill one or two bags with leaves or other soft material and use them like a mattress. It will be softer than the ground and will also provide an insulation layer between you and the ground. If you have an extra bag, fill that also and use it on top of you as additional insulation.

If you need water, use these bags as a means to collect rainwater. If you can, direct run-off water to the bag, such as runs off a shelter or tarp. Or hang one bag like a tarp with one side directing the run-off into another bag.

Again, the uses for garbage bags are only limited by your thought process. Be innovative!

BANDANAS

You should carry at least one bandana and more if room is available. Buy a large one, as they fold down small. Cotton is preferred. I use the old military handkerchief as a bandana; these are 28 inches long x 24 inches wide and fold down fairly small.

First of all, a bandana can be used as a bandana. If it is hot, wet the bandana with water and wear it tied around your neck to keep you cool. If you are sweating, use it as a headband. Wrap one around your head, dew-rag style, for protection from the sun when hot or for protection against heat loss when cold. If your nose is running, use it as a handkerchief. If it is windy or dusty, use it as a nose and mouth cover.

If you need to filter the sediment from water before purifying it, pour it through a bandana. It also works well as a napkin, washcloth, small towel or even a potholder when folded several times. For medical emergencies, it can be used as a bandage, a sling, to tie a splint, etc.

SURGICAL TUBING

Surgical tubing can be obtained from most surgical suppliers and sometimes from a drug store. It is a soft rubber tube that measures approximately 5/16 inch (outside diameter) x 3/16 inch (inside diameter). It is very stretchy, and I carry a piece about 3 feet long in my medium-size kits.

Surgical tubing can be used to make slingshots for obtaining food, as a tourniquet, and as a drinking tube from those small areas where a cup or scoop won't work.

CLEAR PLASTIC TUBING

Clear plastic tubing can be obtained from pet shops that sell fish. It is sometimes called airline tubing for aquariums. The stuff I carry has an outside diameter of approximately 3/16 inch and can be used for obtaining water as indicated above.

BANDANAS / PLASTIC TUBING

ZIP-LOCK BAGS

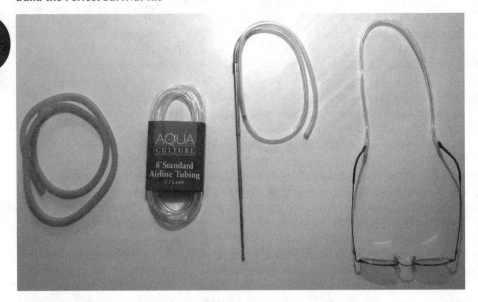

On the left is surgical tubing (which is stretchy). The clear plastic aquarium tubing can be used with a broken antenna for a coal blower or as security for glasses.

I have also used it to blow oxygen into the coals of a fire, which increases the burning temperature. So the tubing doesn't melt, I inserted a small collapsible antenna off a broken radio into the end of the tube. When I want to blow into the coals, I pull the antenna out to its full length and put that end near the coals and blow from the plastic end. When I want to pack it away, I collapse the antenna for compact storage.

This tubing can also be used to secure your glasses. Cut a piece that will fit around your neck and allow the glasses to hang on your chest when not being used. I find this especially helpful, as I am nearsighted and only need my glasses for distance. I normally have them off in camp, as I can't wear them for any close-up activity. Nothing is worse than being out in the wilderness wondering where you laid your glasses. Push the ends of the tubing over the ends of the temples of your glasses. When you aren't wearing them, they can hang down. If you are in a canoe or boat, you can use a shorter piece to secure the glasses directly to your head so they don't fall in the water.

This tubing is very inexpensive, so carry several feet, rolled up, in a medium-size kit.

ZIP-LOCK BAGS

Zip-lock bags, of all shapes and sizes, are vital for building survival kits, as they are great for waterproofing the kits' contents. You can double-bag items for extra protection from moisture, and if you need just the bag while in the field, you simply remove your gear from one.

Zip-lock bags are great containers that fold down small and store easily in extra corners of your kit. Freezer bags are more durable than normal bags, but they also take up more room. These bags can be used to collect or carry water, or to place over the foliage on limbs of trees to collect water through transpiration.

These bags can also quickly become a carrying container in the field. When collecting tinder or food such as berries, they make a convenient means to get those items back to camp. Larger bags can be used to place over your feet when crossing (safe) water such as a creek, etc. They can be used to keep extra clothes dry in the rain or as a bail in a leaky canoe or boat. You should carry various sizes and shapes, as they will prove useful in many situations.

DENTAL FLOSS

Dental floss is a very strong form of thin cordage. It can be used to sew, lash and, in a pinch, floss your teeth. For emergency shoelaces, use several lengths laid together. I have re-wrapped floss onto sewing bobbins for storage and placed them in small plastic tubes. You can even leave it on the spool on which it came. Just take it out of the original container to reduce its size. This is another component that can serve that extra need in an emergency.

SEWING THREAD

Another item that can serve various purposes is sewing thread. Although we already know that dental floss can serve as sewing thread, you may want to carry some heavy-duty sewing thread. Always use nylon/polyester, as it won't rot when it gets wet.

SEWING NEEDLES

Carry several sewing needles with good size eyeholes so you can use sewing thread, dental floss or other thread. Needles make a small package, so pack various sizes. Protect yourself from the points by placing duct tape over the points (which also keeps them from rolling around) or by placing them in a miniature tube or needle holder.

You can magnetize the eye end of your needles before you pack them so they can be used as compass needles. Place a magnetized needle on a leaf and float it in a puddle of water. The point of the needle will face magnetic north.

SEWING AWL

Sewing awls are useful when you have to do some major sewing for repairs. However, the commercial units are rather large and bulky, so I took a sewing awl needle and combined it with the handle from a miniature screwdriver set. The small screwdriver bits were held in the rear of the small tube, which had a screw-on cap. I now store my sewing and awl needles in the rear of the tube. If I need a sewing awl, I take the needle out of the rear tube and use the screwdriver chuck to hold it.

Needle holders: Several needles duct taped to a small piece of cardboard (left), a mini tube with cap to hold needles in a kit (center) and a commercially available needle holder (right).

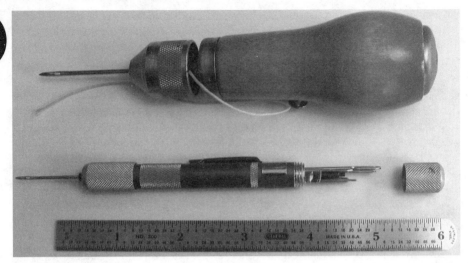

Size comparison of commercial sewing awl to author's, which he made from a miniature screwdriver set.

GLUE STICKS

Glue sticks are small and can be cut down even smaller. They can be used to glue various things by melting the end and then smearing the melted glue on the item. In a survival situation you probably won't have a self-inflating mattress, but hikers and campers can use a glue stick to repair a leak in one of these mattresses.

SAFETY PINS

Safety pins are another item of which you should carry at least a couple different sizes. They can be used to hold clothing together when a button is lost, and they can pin a survival blanket around you or assist in hanging it. One safety pin can be opened and used as a single fishing hook. Three small safety pins can be wired together, back-to-back, to make a treble fishing hook. They can be straightened and used as stiff wire. As with other multi-purpose items, the uses for safety pins are nearly limitless.

FLEXIBLE CABLE TIES

Flexible cable ties are an item that take up hardly any room, yet can be used for various repair and construction tasks. They come in all sizes, so you should be able to find some that will fit most kits including minis. Even in big kits, you should carry various sizes.

Flexible cable ties can be used to attach items to a belt pouch or pack, especially from "D" rings or pack straps. I have even used them to attach a mini spinning reel to a sapling to use it as a fishing pole. Make the eyelets with snare wire as discussed above, and you now have a real (or should I say reel?) fishing pole.

CHAPTER 10

MISCELLANEOUS COMPONENTS

These kit components are made up of those important miscellaneous items that don't fit under any of the other categories. Some of these items may be considered optional, and some are selected based on season or environment.

EXTRA PRESCRIPTION GLASSES

If you wear prescription glasses, you should consider carrying an extra pair in your survival kit. If you are far sighted, you can pick up a pair of the inexpensive mini-folders in various stores. These pack real small and, although not prescription, will work in an emergency. If you are near sighted like me, you need prescription glasses or you just don't see in the distance.

THERMOMETER

As we discussed in Chapter 4, there is a compass with a small thermometer called the Therm-O-Compass. This item, which also has a wind-chill chart, can be hung off the zipper pull of your jacket or pack, and you will always know the temperature.

What I carry in my survival pack is a stream thermometer, which comes in a metal tube with a slot to view the degree markings. It has a metal screw-on cap to hold the thermometer inside, with a small split ring for hanging. They are usually used when fly fishing to determine water temperature, but they will tell you the outside temperature as well. And being stored in a metal tube, it is protected from breakage. It measures 6 inches long x 3/8 inch in diameter. I believe I purchased mine at Orvis, but they are available at most fly-fishing shops.

SURVIVAL MANUAL

Of course, a full-blown manual takes up a lot of room. However, there are various smaller versions of survival manuals that can easily be carried in a survival kit. One that measures only 4 inches x 6 inches x 1/8 inch is the *Emergency/Survival Pocket Guide*. It is a comprehensive, pocket-sized guide that includes sections on Preparation, Surviving in the Wilderness, and Medical Emergencies including trauma. These booklets are available from The Mountaineer Books company.

Another survival guide that fits in small kits is the Survival Cards. This is a compact comprehensive guide displayed on 5-inch x 3-inch laminated cards that are attached in one corner with a small grommet, so they fan open, but stay together. They provide over 150 illustrations and are available at various camping stores such as Campmor and EMS.

There is a nice little laminated book handed out to students at the Wilderness Learning Center. They are 3-5/8 inches x 2-5/8 inches x 3/16 inch. As you read through from one side, it contains comprehensive first-aid information. Read through from the other direction and it provides survival and outback skills. It is packaged very small and will fit in all but a mini kit.

For an all-out survival guide for larger kits, there is the *SAS Survival Guide* by John Wiseman (available at most major book stores and Brigade Quartermasters). This hardcover book, which measures only 4-3/16 inches x 3-3/8 inches x 1 inch, provides a plethora of information and is a good choice for any survival kit big enough to hold it.

KNIFE SHARPENER

For any kit larger than a mini, you can normally fit some type of knife sharpener. Sharpening devices are like knives; everyone has their own preference in type and style. You should carry something to keep an edge on your blade. I prefer small units like the Diamond Mini Sharp made by DMT (Diamond Machining Technology, Inc.), a small triangular sharpener made by LS (Lansky Sharpeners), various rod-type sharpeners that either retract into their own handles or are made for pocket carry, and mini crock-stick configurations. Any of these types of sharpeners can normally fit into one of your kit arrangements.

PENCIL AND WATERPROOF PAPER

Additional items that belong in a survival kit include a pencil and waterproof paper. A pencil can be cut down to a smaller size if need be. You can buy a small pad of waterproof paper called Rite In The Rain at most camping stores or called Stormsaf at Brigade Quartermasters. Available in 3 x 5-inch and 4 x 6-inch spiral-bound tablets, I find the smaller one more suitable for my medium and large kits. For mini kits, you can take several sheets out of the tablet and place them in your kit.

If you decide on a pen as a backup to the pencil (always carry the pencil), a Fisher Bullet Space Pen is a good choice. The pen is 5-3/8 inches long when open but only 3-7/8 inches long when closed. I have carried one of these in my pocket for over 15 years. This pen writes upside down, underwater, over grease or in any weather. It has a hermetically sealed nitrogen-pressurized ink cartridge with an ultra-hard, tungsten-carbide ball tip.

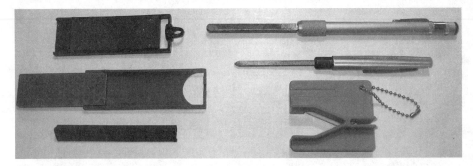

The top left sharpener shown here is a Diamond Mini Sharp in the folded position. The one below it is the same in the open position. The bottom left is a Lansky triangular sharpener with the rubber ends removed to decrease its size. The top right is a Gerber retractable rod sharpener, with a small pocket sharpener under it. The right bottom is a mini crock stick.

TOILET PAPER

Toilet paper is a convenience item that is your option. It can also be used for tinder, so a small amount is not a bad thing. Obviously, you don't want to carry a normal bathroom roll. There are some smaller rolls at camp stores. Also, in the travel section of some drugstores, there are small rolls in a little dispenser, which can be fine for larger kits. If you want to place some in a smaller kit, you can easily re-roll it on itself so the center tube is eliminated, thus reducing the size of the finished package.

CELL PHONE

A cell phone can be a wonderful survival device, if you have cell coverage in the area in which you are operating. In the Adirondacks of New York, they work in some places and not in others. If you carry one, keep it in a small waterproof pouch to protect it from the elements.

In regard to batteries, as with many other things, carry extra if possible. I carry a Motorola StarTAC (yes, a little old fashion – but my preference for size) and have located replacement battery cases that actually hold three AAA batteries. I always carry extra AAA, as all my flashlights use them, but that also means I always have power for my cell phone.

SEASONAL AND ENVIRONMENTALLY SPECIFIC ITEMS

The basic contents of your mini kit always remain the same. However, seasonal or environmental factors can change the contents of a larger kit. The clothes you carry for a summer outing will differ from those for a winter trip. If you are making a large kit that will stay in a vehicle, you must take this in to consideration. You should plan for the worst and be prepared for any season.

Environmental considerations must also be taken into account. Based on whether you will most likely be in a desert or swamp environment, certain items will differ. An example might be carrying a machete as the blade of choice as opposed to a smaller knife. If you are going to be in a snow environment, some other specific items might be included such as snowshoes, collapsible snow shovel, metal canteen or a snow-melting stove.

Of course, we cannot always predict where or when we might end up in a survival situation. But giving some thought to the matter before leaving on an adventure or vacation is always a good idea. You should make a point to never be caught without the proper equipment for the season or environment. Of course, this doesn't apply when you are thrust into a truly unexpected survival situation, such as a plane crash. Although you should at least have your mini kit in this situation.

Now that we have completed the first two parts of the book, it is time to move on to the part you have been waiting for! Part Three will teach you how to actually make the survival kits the earlier chapters have been alluding to all along. Yes, they really do exist; so let's get started!

103

TOILET PAPER / CELL PHONE / SEASONAL ITEMS

PART THREE — THE KITS

CHAPTER 11
SELECTING CONTAINERS FOR SURVIVAL KITS

Now that we understand the components required to make a survival kit, let's discuss how we can package our own kits. Before we do, however, you should understand that you, yourself, can be the first line of defense in a survival situation. What I mean here is that YOU can be the container! You can carry items on your person, in pockets or on your belt, that supplement a survival kit. There are certain items that go in my pockets and on my belt everyday. It doesn't matter if I plan on going anywhere or if I'm sitting home writing. If an emergency occurs, I know I always have these minimal items on me.

First, as I guess you've already suspected, I always (I mean always) have at least one knife on me. You already know this is my top choice for a component if I could only carry one. In my left front pocket, I always have a small flashlight (the UKE Mini Pocket Light discussed in Chapter 2) and a wind-proof lighter. I also carry my key ring (the one with the truck keys) in this pocket. It includes a white-light Photon Micro-Light II and a small stainless-steel vial with an "O"-ring-sealed, screw-on cap that holds 2 aspirin and 6 Advil tablets. This small vial measures 2-3/8 inches long by 1/2 inch in diameter and has a ring attached to the top.

In my right front pocket, I always have my other key ring, which doesn't have keys on it. Instead, it has another stainless-steel vial, as described above, which holds several Tinder-Quick Fire Tabs (as discussed in Chapter 2). It also carries my folding hacksaw, a Leatherman Micra tool, a Mini-Match magnesium/flint stick, a Hot-Spark flint, a striker, a red-light Photon Micro-Light II, a

The author's everyday-carry items – left side shows what's carried on the left side of his body and right, the right side.

small Fox 40 whistle that has been slightly modified to make it smaller and a small bearing (for use with a fire bow and drill) made from deer antler. I also carry my Space pen and a lighter in this pocket.

My left rear pocket carries my wallet, which has a Fresnel magnifier in it, as well as a color copy of my passport. My right rear pocket always has a small bandana folded up in it.

On my belt, I carry my Gerber multi-tool in a belt pouch. As you can see, I am readily prepared even if I don't have a mini or larger kit on me. Of course, one day when I was emptying my pockets in a gym for a class on executive protection defensive tactics, the students were warned not to stand next to me in a lightning storm!

For sure, I have been known to carry other items, but these are my everyday basics. I never have to wonder what I am carrying, as I always carry the same things, as a minimum. You may wonder why I carry a mini kit at all, but as I've said before, I am a man of redundancy (not anal retentive as my wife would have you believe).

However, not everybody is like me, nor do they take survival as serious as me. For those people, we have already established they should carry a survival kit. So let's get started.

CHOOSING THE RIGHT CONTAINER

The first step is to determine what size kit we want to build. Do you want a mini kit? Or maybe a small belt-carried kit, or a fanny-pack kit might be more suitable for your needs. Maybe a mini kit on you and a medium-sized one in a separate container?

Decide on the individual components you want to carry. Remember from Chapter 1, you should include at least one from each major group and two or more from some of the groups. If you are building small, then select the smallest items that will perform the functions desired. As an example, if you are trying to build a kit in a small Altoids tin, then don't choose the larger Doan Magnesium Firestarter, as it will take up a third of the tin. Choose the smaller Mini-Match instead. Go through each component group and base your decisions on your size limitations. As the size of your kit grows, so can the size of the components.

Be innovative. Repackage items for the smallest size and, whenever possible, select items that can perform more than one function. As I have stated over and over, multi-purpose is a good thing!

Once you decide on the approximate size of your components, you must decide in what you are going to carry them. Choosing the right container also involves more questions. Do you want it in a tin, a soft package or a waterproof container? Try to make these decisions before you start.

TINS

Small tins have often been selected as containers for small survival kits. One of their advantages is you can cook in them. Although many of the real small ones won't boil a lot of water, they will allow you to make some tea. If you select a tin, try to find one in the configuration you desire. Some are sized for your pants pocket, some will fit in a vest or jacket pocket, some are flat and some are high. Experiment with different configurations before making a decision. I have often chosen one container over another only because it fit perfectly in the spot I wanted it to fit.

PLASTIC CONTAINERS

A small selection of tins from the author's collection. All of these tins have a one-piece bottom. They can be selected for size and shape, depending on your personal kit requirements.

You can find tins in various places. Of course, the Altoids tin can be found almost everywhere. But you should look closer. There are other mints that come in tins of various shapes (I don't like mints, but you would never know it with the amount of mint tins I have bought!). Tobacco tins have also been a favorite for survival kits but are becoming harder to find (of course, so is tobacco). Candy samplers also come in tins sometimes. Flea markets are another place to find tins. Be careful at antique booths, though, as they often look at tins as an expensive collectible; we are just looking for a kit container. Keep your eyes open and you'll be surprised at what you might find. I collect differently sized tins whenever I find them and store them in a plastic bin. When I need a tin for a kit, I just check my own collection first.

Be careful with some tins, as they have false bottoms. This describes a tin with a bottom that has been pressed in, which leaves an unsealed seam around the bottom. If you try to cook in this type of tin, it will leak. Choose tins that have a one-piece bottom and sides. This type uses one piece of tin for the bottom, and the bottom is pressed in with a large press. The top is a separate piece and fits onto the bottom tightly. Sometimes there are small pressed hinges as part of the tin. This is your preference. I don't normally care if it has hinges, as long as it has a one-piece bottom and fits the size I'm seeking.

Once you make your kit, seal the lid to the bottom by wrapping some Scotch 33+ electrical tape (this is the best, as you can put it on and take it off many times and it will still stick) around the place where the lid meets the bottom. This will help to keep the kit watertight.

PLASTIC CONTAINERS

Some people prefer packaging their small survival kit in a plastic case. It can still be used to collect water but can't be placed over a fire. Your aluminum foil can always make a cup or pot.

If you choose plastic, try to find a container that has a lid, such as a travel soap dish or cigarette case. There are some hard plastic boxes with lids, but be careful. Some are not very sturdy and are easily broken. One that comes to mind is the clear plastic box used to store baseball-card collections. It is very brittle. One that

SOFT CASES

Various plastic containers appropriate for a small survival kit. At top left is the Huggies Baby Wipes case and at top right is the personal decontamination-kit case. The second clear box from the right, bottom row, is the anti-snakebite serum case, with the Mighty TUFF box above it.

is very durable is the Mighty TUFF parts box sold in the Jensen Tools catalog. It has small rust-resistant metal hinges, is unbreakable, and is highly resistant to oil, gasoline, and most chemicals and solvents. Although most have little dividers built in, one sized at 4-3/8 inches long x 2-5/8 inches wide x 1-1/16 inches high does not have dividers and is ideal for a small kit.

A very durable plastic box I used for a mini kit was made to hold anti-snakebite serum. The lid fits tightly onto the bottom and it fit nicely in the case I was using for my kit. A little tape around the seam made it watertight.

Another plastic container that is great for small kits is an old personal decontamination-kit case. I used to find these at flea markets, but they are now available (the case only) from Brigade Quartermasters. They have a waterproof snap lid and measure 4-1/4 inches high x 2-7/8 inches wide x 1-7/8 inches deep. They even have a clip on the side to hang it on your belt or attach it to a small pack.

If you wanted to make a medium-sized kit in a plastic container that would store in the large pocket of a jacket or vest, try a Huggies Baby Wipes case (I don't have children, but when I go to the grocery store with my wife, I spend my time looking for various containers, or food items, that would be appropriate for survival). This container is 8-1/8 inches long x 4-1/4 inches wide x only 1 inch thick. This type of container can also be used to house your small kit of essentials and stored in the bottom of a small pack or even your vehicle. You could supplement it with larger items.

The idea here is to keep your eyes open for containers. They can and will be found when you least expect it. I once used the slim plastic case for some miniature rum-dipped cigars as a container for a mini kit. It slipped very nicely right into a shirt pocket.

SOFT CASES

I break soft cases down into small, medium and large kits. Small soft kits would normally be worn on the belt or carried on your person, possibly in a large pocket. A medium-size kit will normally be in a fanny pack or a small case that can be carried slung over one shoulder. A large kit would go in a small to large backpack or carry bag.

For small kits that will be belt worn or placed in a pack or other container, you may want a small soft case. Sometimes I have built a mini kit in a tin and placed it in a soft case with supplemental items like a survival blanket and poncho. Like I've said before, keep an open mind and think outside the box.

There are a multitude of small soft cases and pouches from which to choose. They can be found at camp stores, luggage shops or military suppliers to mention but a few. From small belt pouches to mini waist pouches and packs, New Sun Productions is a company that specializes in small cases and pouches for the adventurer. They are very innovative and have a good selection. Brigade Quartermasters has two pages devoted to small belt-worn pouches. Outdoor Research, already mentioned in Chapter 8, also has a nice selection of organizer-type soft pouches.

Some of these small pouches have various pockets and compartments with zippers or velcro closures. These allow you to segregate different components in different areas if you want. Fire starting and knives can go in one compartment, signaling and navigation in another, and so forth. You can make it as simple or elaborate as you desire.

A nice soft case for a small survival kit is made by Spec-Ops Brand and is called the "On-Board Dry-Cell Organizer." Specifically designed to fit into the leg pocket of BDU (Battle Dress Utilities) trousers, which I often wear in the field, this case works fine for me. With the inside divided into two sections, it measures 7-1/2 inches x 7 inches x 1 inch and has a zipper at the top along with a small pull loop to extract the pouch easily from the BDU leg pocket. It provides you with two Aloksak element-proof bags, which fit inside, to protect the contents from water and moisture. A three-slot mesh pocket, designed not to snag, has been sewn on

 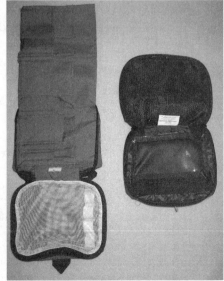

The left photo shows several small belt-worn cases made by New Sun Productions (the case on right can be worn on the belt or slung over the shoulder). The photo on right has two organizer pouches made by Outdoor Research.

Two shoulder-slung bags at left and one fanny pack on right in which a nice medium-size survival kit could be packed.

The author's long-term survival pack at left and vehicle kit bag at right.

the outside of one side for extra storage of a flashlight, pen, pocket tool, knife, etc. This pouch also has belt loops for conventional wear on a belt, as well as ALICE-clip attachment points for attaching to military packs.

There are also pouches that have built-in organizer pallets, as I showed in Chapter 8 with a medical kit inside. Made by Outdoor Research, they allow you to see all your components when the pallets are unfolded. The cases come in various sizes, and I will show a kit built in one of these small cases under small-sized survival kits.

There are various mini fanny packs or pouches that can be used for a small kit. Some of them hold the pouch to your side and are very light.

Whatever type of case you choose, make sure it is durable, water repellent and able to take a beating. After all, once you finish this book and build your own kit, you will be wearing it everywhere.

Medium soft cases also come in various shapes and sizes. For medium-sized kits, I try to find a case that will allow me to carry it slung over one shoulder, or I make it in a small fanny pack so it can be worn unobtrusively.

I normally choose bags to be slung over a shoulder that are in the size area of 6 to 8 inches wide x 8 to 10 inches high x 4 to 6 inches deep. They can be one big pouch if I am going to carry a small kit in conjunction with supplemental items like a large survival blanket and water bottle or canteen. If the pouch itself will be my kit, I prefer various sections for storing different components so they are easy to find.

A small fanny pack can be a good container for a medium-size kit because they normally accommodate one or two water bottles on the outside, and some of the newer ones are even small hydration units. You can pack your survival kit inside, have water for hydration, possibly have additional room for some extra clothes, and wear it comfortably on your waist.

WATERPROOF CONTAINERS

The type and configuration should be something with which you are comfortable and that allows you to pack the components you desire.

Large soft cases are usually reserved for long-term survival but can also be used for vehicle or aircraft kits. I use a large soft bag for my vehicle kit but a small pack for my long-term survival kit. This is the pack I use for up to 10 days when in the field for survival courses and excursions.

WATERPROOF CONTAINERS

We have already discussed tins, plastic cases, and small, medium and large soft cases. But what if you want your kit to be waterproof? Maybe your kit is for a boat, or you're planning water-borne activities such as canoeing.

You can use a soft waterproof pouch to house your mini kits. There are various sized pouches for small kits and large soft waterproof bags to house a medium or large survival kit as well as additional equipment. These waterproof pouches and bags are available at most camping or marine stores.

There are many types of large waterproof bags made for water activities. Many of them roll down from the top and are attached with Fastex-type fasteners to keep the bag closed. These are good for medium to large kits and the sizes are staggering. I have one called the Boundary Pack that fits my entire long-term survival pack and provides additional shoulder straps so the entire package can be carried. There are also some bags that have a diagonal zipper across the top; SealLine manufactures most of these.

If you want a waterproof survival kit, but you know it will take a beating, you may want to consider a hard case. Available in just about every size and shape imaginable from manufacturers like Otter Box, Pelican Cases and Underwater Kinetics, these cases are built extremely tough out of ABS plastic and include an "O"-ring seal in the lid. The Pelican and Underwater Kinetics cases actually have a purge valve to equalize the

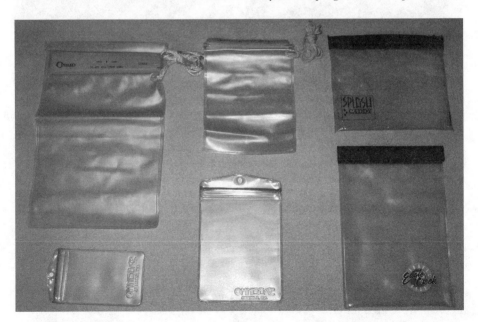

Various waterproof pouches that could be used for mini and small kits.

WATERPROOF CONTAINERS

All three of these bags – a large diagonal zippered waterproof bag on left and a solid color and clear roll-down waterproof bag on right – are made by SealLine.

These smaller, hard waterproof boxes are ideal for small survival kits.

Any one of these hard waterproof cases would be adequate for a medium or large survival kit.

pressure inside, so they can be opened after changes in altitude or temperature. I have often had to use this valve after a flight in order to open the case.

This should provide us with a good idea of the types of containers available for building survival kits. They can be small, medium or large. They can be placed in tins, in plastic containers, in various soft containers, or in various soft or hard waterproof containers. Pick one and let's get started on building your own survival kit.

CHAPTER 12

MAKING MINI and SMALL KITS

This chapter describes how to actually make mini and small survival kits. Components are selected and then packaged for the smallest kit size. When you are done with this chapter, you should have no problem planning, picking the components for, and packaging your own mini or small survival kit.

MAKING MINI KITS

Mini kits are the easiest to carry, so you should never have an excuse not to carry one. On the other hand, they provide the least amount of survival equipment. Therefore, you must select your components wisely, always looking for the smallest size and multi-purpose features.

In the last chapter on container selection, we discussed how you can be the actual container for a mini kit. By carrying various survival components on your person, you already have something in the event of an emergency. If you carry these items as a daily habit, they can essentially be eliminated from a separate mini kit, or the kit can have duplicate items of a smaller size. In Chapter 6, I also introduced you to my survival hat, which provides me with those extra items I don't always carry on me.

Aluminum-Foil Mini Kit

The first kit we will build is what I call the aluminum-foil mini kit because we use aluminum foil as the actual container. This keeps the kit small and flat so it can even be carried in a shirt pocket. It also provides you with an appropriate amount of aluminum foil for making a cup, collecting water or signaling.

We start by adding fire components: a Mini-Match miniature magnesium/flint bar and a striker. I also add one layer of book matches that have been removed from a book and coated with Thompson's Water Seal to waterproof them (I normally like to use regular waterproof stick matches, but to keep the kit thin, I went this way). I also cut the striker off the book of matches and add that. Several cotton balls coated with petroleum jelly are added by twisting them tightly in a small roll with Saran Wrap. Two alcohol prep pads are included, which can also be used as fire starters. A cut-down Fresnel magnifier is incorporated for an additional fire starter and as a multi-purpose device.

For the signaling component, you have the aluminum foil. For navigation, I used an ultra-small compass capsule and magnetized needles. For water, you can use the aluminum foil to collect the water and then boil it for purification. For food, I added two fishhooks and two swivels, which I taped to the back of an alcohol prep pad. I also wrapped 30 feet of 12-lb. fishing line around a flat floss bobbin. Four split shot, one fishing leader, which can also be used as a snare, and snare wire were also added.

For first aid, I have two alcohol prep pads, two butterfly closures and one packet of antibiotic ointment. For miscellaneous components, I use two safety pins

Build the Perfect Survival Kit

and two needles (magnetized as indicated earlier) taped to the back of the second alcohol prep pad.

I add one small Swiss Army knife with one blade, one small pair of scissors, a small file, tweezers and tooth pick. Now fold the heavy-duty aluminum foil (a couple of feet) so that it provides a finished size of about 3-5/8 inches x 2-1/4 inches when folded. Unfold the foil and use one of the center 3-5/8-inch x 2-1/4-inch sections as a small pocket-type dish to load all the above components. You may have to bend the sides a bit so the chosen section is like a little square dish. Then refold the aluminum foil, being careful to keep all the components in that one section. When all is said and done, the package should measure about 3-5/8 inches long x 2-1/4 inches wide x 3/8 inch thick.

This kit should fulfill the basic needs of a survival situation and yet is small and light enough to carry on you anytime and anywhere.

Congratulations! You have just learned how to make your first personal survival kit. It probably was not as hard as you might have expected. We simply started with the basics and added at least one item from each component section (except the shelter and protection section). An item from this component could include a small survival blanket and emergency poncho carried in another pocket.

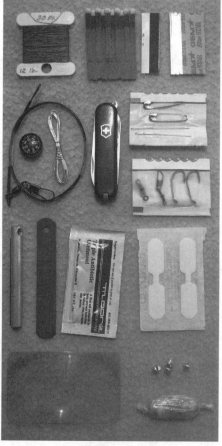

The components for the aluminum-foil mini kit are shown at right. The top photo shows the components all laid into one of the 3-5/8 x 2-1/4-inch folded sections. The bottom photo above has the complete mini kit all folded and ready for carrying. Note a section of bicycle inner tube was used as a rubber band to hold the kit together.

The thin cigar case when closed and shown open with all the components from the aluminum-foil mini kit inside. One foot of aluminum foil was tightly folded and placed inside to replace the foil used as the container in the first kit.

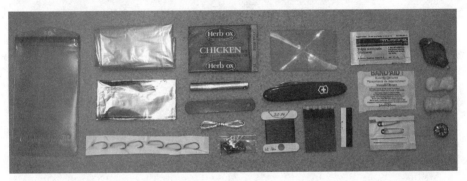

The individual components of the mini survival kit built into a small waterproof pouch. Some components were changed from the first two kits, but ultimately, the changes provided better items, while losing only one.

Cigar-Case Mini Kit

The components used for the above mini kit can be used for other configurations as well. They can all be placed in a hard plastic case, for example, to provide a little more durability. The hard case from the rum-soaked mini cigars, as described in the Selecting Containers chapter, is a good choice. This little case, 3-1/2 inches wide x 3-1/2 inches high x 1/2 inch thick, has a small fold-open section at top (for the removal of the original cigars) and was designed to be carried in a shirt pocket. All the items outlined above in the aluminum-foil kit were easily placed within this container. I was also able to add one packet of chicken bouillon as an addition to the food section. Of course, the amount of aluminum foil was reduced to one square foot, tightly folded and slid inside the container, but you can still signal and make a small cup. Even if the aluminum foil didn't fit inside, you could wrap the case in foil, or carry it with a small survival blanket and emergency poncho. However, if I were carrying this kit, I would already be covered with my hat (no pun intended), as I always have the flat roll of aluminum foil under the brim (described in Chapter 6).

Waterproof-Pouch Mini Kit

The next mini kit will be built inside a small waterproof pouch. A small license holder that measures 4-1/2 inches long x 2-3/4 inches wide and that will easily

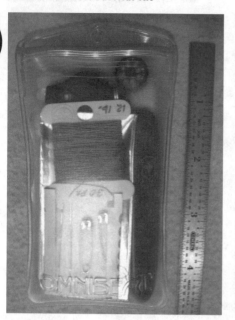 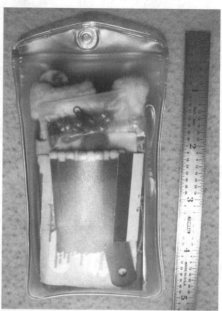

The front side of the waterproof mini kit is on the left and the backside is on the right.

fit in a shirt pocket is a good choice for this kit. Some of the components will remain the same, but some will change.

With all things, there are trade-offs. I wanted to add a larger, two-blade knife (one 2-1/8-inch blade and one 1-1/8-inch blade), a flashlight (I used a Photon Micro-Light II as described in Chapter 2) and a mini water bag (see Chapter 5) to hold 2 quarts of water. I wanted to replace the petroleum cotton balls with two Tinder-Quick Fire Tabs (see Chapter 2) and add a bouillon packet and aluminum foil (1 foot of heavy-duty).

The fishing tackle was increased to six fishing hooks, six split shot and four snap swivels. The only thing I had to delete to add these additional components was the fishing leader. I thought it was a good trade, and if I wanted to take a chance of bursting the seams on the waterproof case, I may have been able to fit that in also.

Altoids-Tin Mini Kit

You can choose any size tin you want, and there are certainly larger ones, but let's see what we can get in a tin measuring only 3-3/4 inches long x 2-3/8 inches wide x 3/4 inch thick.

For fire and light components, I again selected the Mini-Match magnesium fire starter with striker, six waterproof/wind-proof Lifeboat matches with a striker (placed in a mini zip-lock bag, then rolled and taped) and five Tinder-Quick Fire Tabs. A Fresnel magnifier, a candle cut down to fit the tin and a Photon Micro-Light II were also selected.

For the signaling component, I wanted a signal mirror, but they were all too thick, taking up too much room in the tin. So I custom-made one on an ultra-thin piece of plastic (it's called super mica and is used by locksmiths to slide between the door and jamb to push the latch back). I glued a piece of thin mirror-finish

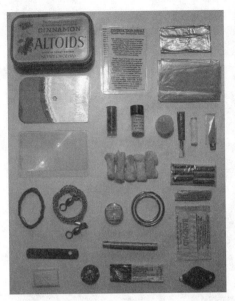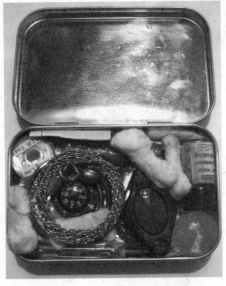

The Altoids tin packed (right) and with all the components laid out for review (left).

material to this plastic and used a leather punch to make a sighting hole. Rounding the corners so it fit in the bottom of the tin, the completed mirror is only 1/32 of an inch thick. For the navigation component, I used a button compass.

For the water and food component, I chose a mini water bag (as described in Chapter 5) and 2 feet of tightly folded aluminum foil. I also repacked 20 Potable Aqua water-purification tablets in a mini glass vial (again, see Chapter 5). I added a fishing tackle kit in a small plastic tube measuring only 1-3/16 inches tall x 7/16 inches in diameter. It contains 12 assorted hooks, six swivels and six split shot. Twenty feet of fishing line wound on a sewing bobbin was added, as well as some snare wire.

I again left out a shelter and protection component, as I always carry a mini survival blanket along with this kit. I also always have parachute cord on my hat, walking stick and elsewhere, so I didn't include it either. If you don't carry it as a norm, you could wrap the Altoids tin with some when the kit is completed.

For knife and tools, I decided to trade the size of a knife for a survival saw and just add a couple of razor-knife blades (I think we have established I always carry a knife). For medical components, I selected a packet of triple antibiotic ointment and two butterfly closures. For multi-purpose/miscellaneous components, some nylon string, a glue stick, and laminated instructions for the Potable Aqua and Fishing Knots were included.

The result of packing all these components in the tin is a very serviceable mini survival kit. To keep the completed kit from rattling, the Tinder-Quick Fire Tabs can be stuffed in various corners and open spots.

Bamboo Walking Stick Mini Kit

This mini kit will use a bamboo walking stick as the container. I wanted to use a bamboo pole for the walking stick because I usually use one anyway, and they are very strong and extremely light. They can usually be found at garden

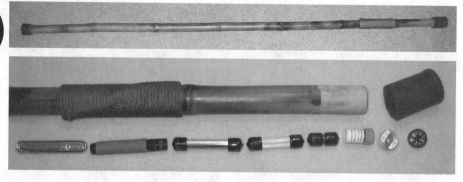

The completed walking stick is shown above the components lined up for insertion.

The components of the bamboo-stick kit with the button compass at the top of the stack, ready for the rubber top closure cap.

shops (people use them for bean poles) and are usually inexpensive. If you know anything about bamboo, you will already know my last reason for selecting bamboo. There are large diameter rings every so often along the length of the stick; these are the growth rings. They are solid, but the sections in between these rings are hollow. Why not use these hollow sections to accommodate a mini survival kit? Keep in mind when you use a bamboo pole for a walking stick, you want a growth ring at both the top and the bottom so the ends are sturdy and tough.

The walking stick I selected is 5 feet tall by approximately 1-1/4 inches in diameter at the sectional dividers and slightly less in between. Be careful when selecting a bamboo stick. If you buy one that is the height you want, it will probably be too small in diameter. Rather, pick a stick with the approximate diameter you desire, and then cut it down to the length you want, being careful to cut it at a growth ring. I also lightly sanded mine and applied a coat of stain (just for looks).

The first thing I did was drill open one end with a 9/16-inch bit, as this was the size I needed for my component tubes and other items. This just also happened to be the approximate inside diameter of the hollow sections (sometimes I do get lucky). The length of the first section to the first growth ring was too short for the components I wanted to place inside, so I had to drill through the next growth ring to open the next hollow section. I would not advise going through another, as you will begin to lose the structural integrity of the pole. Also be careful as to the diameter of the hole you drill inside. You want to maintain the existing inside diameter of the hollow section. If you start to remove material in the hollow section, it will become weak and the pole will split.

I wanted the button compass and sewing bobbin, on which I had wound 40 feet of 20-lb braided fishing line, to sit just inside the top of the pole. Also, the button compass and sewing bobbin were 3/4 inch in diameter (the hollow section was only 9/16 inch) and together they were 3/4 inch high. I made the decision to drill the top of the pole 13/16 inch in diameter, but only 3/4 inch down. As I was only drilling down this amount through the solid growth ring, I didn't feel the structural integrity would be reduced all that much. Now when I fed the component tubes inside the 9/16-inch hollow section, there would be a little ledge for the sewing bobbin and the compass to sit. They would then fit flush to the top of the pole, with the compass on top of the sewing bobbin.

As for the components I put inside, for fire and light, I again selected the Mini-Match miniature magnesium/flint bar (it is still the smallest I can find). However, the steel striker that I normally carry with it was too wide to fit inside the clear tube (I use clear plastic tubes with end caps to hold the different component groups; they can be purchased from Brownells gun parts catalog). Instead I selected a small saber-saw blade and ground off the back for a sharp edge to strike the flint. This also left the saw for minor sawing duties (a multi-purpose device). Several small cotton balls with petroleum jelly were rolled tightly into Saran wrap and tucked in the end of the tube. For light, a Mini-Mag AAA-battery Solitaire flashlight fit inside the hollow section of the pole nicely.

For signaling, nothing fit in the pole, so I would have to rely on the Fox 40 whistle that always resides on my supplemental key ring. For navigation, as mentioned earlier, I used a 20 mm liquid-filled button compass with a highly luminous dial.

For water and food, I included a small glass vial with 20 Potable Aqua water-purification tablets (see Chapter 5 for information on glass vial). I also selected a non-lubricated condom, as the water bag I normally use would not fit in this configuration. I placed it inside a clear plastic tube with end caps. A fishing kit with eight #8 hooks, two #6 hooks, six split shot and four mini snap swivels was placed in another plastic tube with end caps. Forty feet of 20-lb. braided fishing line was rewound on a sewing bobbin and labeled.

For shelter and protection, parachute cord for building a shelter was wrapped around the handle of the walking stick. A large plastic garbage bag can also be wrapped around the handle first, with the parachute cord wrapped over it. This would provide further protection as a rain poncho or small shelter. The parachute cord also provides other uses as discussed in Chapter 6.

For knives and tools, a Christy survival knife (see Chapter 7), which fit nicely inside the hollow tube of the pole, was selected. I also had the previously discussed saber-saw blade.

For medical emergencies, I wrapped a small amount of duct tape around the flashlight to provide me with a means to close a small laceration or other wound.

Keep in mind that I measured the depth of the hollow section before I started to select components. I then worked with various options to find the items that would fit that length. I also had to take in consideration the depth of the end caps for the clear plastic tubing. Sounds easy, but it took several hours to complete the selection. Once all the components were packaged, they were checked inside the hollow section of the pole to ensure they would slide in and out easily without getting stuck.

Once the components were packaged and placed inside, a lid was needed to secure them. I had already used a rubber chair leg tip to protect the end that

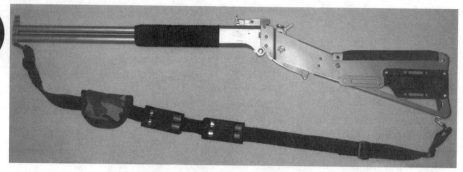

A view of the author's M6-Survival Rifle converted into a mini survival kit.

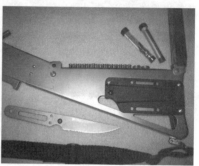

A view (on left) of the parachute cord wrapped around the two barrels and the small pouch attached to the sling. There are also 4 extra shotgun rounds on the sling in dual loop holders. The right photo shows the hinged top cover open on the stock, with the two tubes that hold fire-starting and fishing kits. The knife is shown removed from the sheath that was screwed to the stock so it could be removed.

comes in contact with the ground; I didn't want the same thing on top. So the search was on. Finally, the light bulb went on, and a motorcycle shop was the next stop. I located a replacement handlebar grip for a Harley-Davidson that was a soft yet pliable rubber. Back in the shop, all but the last two inches were cut off. The remaining 2-inch piece slides on easily, holds the components securely and fits tightly. This was just what I wanted for an end cap on my walking-stick mini kit.

Before moving on to small kits, I want to mention that sometimes a mini kit does not have to be complete in regard to all required component groups. As shown here, a mini kit is limited in space, and you often have to supplement it with a survival blanket, etc. I have also built mini kits already knowing what other components I will carry on my person. I call these supplemental mini kits, fully knowing ahead of time they will need other components to be complete.

Rifle Mini Kit

This mini kit was built using an M6-Scout Survival Rifle as the container. This rifle was originally designed as a survival rifle for the U.S. Air Force. I have not discussed survival weapons, as they are even more controversial than knives. This rifle/shotgun happens to be my favorite because it provides me with a 22-caliber rifle as well as a .410 shotgun, each one having its use in a survival situation. Let's see how I converted it into a survival kit.

First of all, I wanted it to have parachute cord, so I wrapped the front of the barrels with two rows of it, which also provided a soft fore-grip for holding the rifle. It should be noted that before you do this you must first put a small block between the two barrels, so that when you wrap it with the parachute cord, it does not pull the two barrels together, bending them. I used a small block of aluminum filed down to the proper size and then duct taped it in place while I wrapped the barrels.

Next, I wanted a knife to stay with the weapon, so I used a CRKT MDP Stiff Kiss, as described in Chapter 7. At first I was going to epoxy the Kydex sheath to the stock of the weapon but thought I might want to be able to take the knife off and wear it separately in a survival situation. Instead, I screwed the sheath to the stock. Now I can leave it on the weapon or take it off and carry it.

I also wanted the weapon to provide me with fire-starting, fishing and water-purification capabilities. There is a section under a hinged top cover on the stock that holds 14 extra 22 cartridges and four shotgun rounds. I decided to remove two of the extra shotgun rounds and use those two round compartments for fire-starting and fishing kits. I built each in a small plastic tube the same length and diameter as a .410-shotgun round. The fire-starting kit has a Mini-Match magnesium/flint bar and a striker made from a saber-saw blade, as described under the bamboo walking-stick kit. The fishing kit has 20 feet of fishing line, hooks, split shot and swivels. Each tube slides into one of the former shotgun-round compartments and resides under the hinged cover.

A space was needed for water-purification tablets, repackaged in a mini glass vial (see Chapter 5), and aluminum foil to make a cup and for signaling. I had added a sling to the weapon and decided to sew a small pouch on the sling for this purpose. As it worked out, the pouch accommodated the vial of water-purification tablets and the aluminum foil, and I still had room for a survival wire saw and two extra shotgun rounds (the two I lost under the hinged stock cover). It also provided room for a small plastic container with 20 extra 22 cartridges. I felt some extra shotgun rounds would be useful, so I sewed two dual-capacity loops onto the sling.

The finished product provides me with protection, food collection (the weapon and fishing), fire starting, signaling (the weapon and the aluminum foil), water

 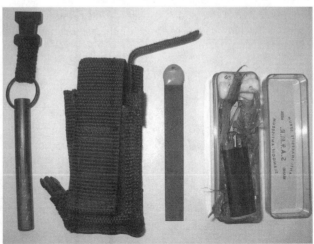

The belt pouch for a supplemental fire kit includes the items shown here.

The snake-serum case open with the Curly Birch, lighter, six Tinder-Quick Fire Tabs, magnesium bar with flint, shaved-down candle and extra striker.

purification, and parachute cord and a survival wire saw to build a shelter. Not bad for an item that I carry anyway on long-term survival trips.

Some mini kits can even be specific. I carry a small pouch on my belt when in the field that is just a fire-starting kit. On one side of the belt pouch is a small divider to hold a 4-inch x 1/2-inch flint with a split ring and Fastex fastener to secure it to the side of the pouch. A flat file that is 4-3/4 inches long x 9/16 inch wide x 1/8 inch thick and that was cut off a longer shop file fits in a divider on the other side of the pouch and is secured with a Velcro flap. This file is also a multi-purpose item, as it can be used as a striker for the flint or to sharpen my larger knives. You will notice that if an item hangs off my belt I always ensure it is double secured with an additional fastener, as you simply can't afford to lose an item in the field.

The center of the pouch carries a used plastic snake-serum case that I use to store six Tinder-Quick Fire Tabs, a lighter, a magnesium block with additional

On the left is the mini belt-pouch kit open, showing the contents. On the right is the mini belt pouch on the author's belt in front of the fire-starter pouch described earlier.

striker, a candle cut to fit, and as much Curly Birch (a great tinder) as will fit, to ensure I always have some dry tinder to start a fire.

Another supplemental kit I made was placed in the same type of small pouch I used on the sling of the M6-Scout survival rifle. I will sometimes wear this when hiking, with a knife. It provides me with a wire survival saw, Tinder-Quik Fire Tabs, a good size fishing kit built into a mini Altoids tin (the contents can be seen in Chapter 5), aluminum foil, a Mini-Match magnesium/flint bar, a striker and eight waterproof strike-anywhere matches. The Mini-Match and matches are stored in a neat little metal match case I picked up at a flea market. It even has a striker for matches on the bottom of the case.

MAKING SMALL KITS

Now that we have an idea how to make various mini survival kits, let's build some slightly larger kits. Since small survival kits provide you with more room than a mini kit, you can either add larger components or more components of a smaller size.

Small Kit #1 in Small Tin & Belt-Pouch Kit

The first small kit we will examine is made inside a tin (larger than an Altoids tin) placed inside a belt pouch with supplemental items. Together, all the components make up a complete survival kit.

I started with a belt pouch that measures 6 inches wide x 4 inches high x 2 inches thick. Both the lid and the inside have a zippered compartment. The tin I used was an old tin from a repair kit for a waxed coat. With a removable lid with a rubber seal on the inside, it measures 4-3/8 inches long x 3-1/4 inches wide x 1-1/16 inches high. I now had my two containers and was ready to select the components.

For fire and light, I selected a Mini-Match magnesium/flint rod with striker, 12 Lifeboat waterproof/wind-proof matches (in a small zip-lock bag rolled and taped), a small BIC lighter, a tub candle and six Tinder-Quik Fire Tabs. These were placed in the tin, and I added a CMG Infinity LED Task Light (as described in Chapter 2) inside the belt pouch. A little overkill on the fire and light, but I had the room.

For signaling, a StarFlash Mirror (as described in Chapter 3) was added to the tin. For navigation, a large fixed-dial compass was chosen. For water and food, a small glass vial of Potable Aqua was included, as well as a matching vial of P.A. Plus, an item

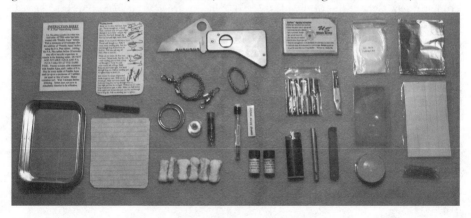

Here are the contents from the survival tin used in Small Kit #1, as described in the text, with the addition of the knife, shown in the open position.

manufactured by WPC to neutralize the taste of the iodine. A small water bag was also folded and added in the bottom of the tin. Fifty feet of 12-lb. fishing line was included with a fishing tackle tube containing hooks, split shot and swivels. Aluminum foil was included to make a cup and for cooking. A roll of snare wire was also added.

For shelter and protection, a survival blanket and emergency poncho were packed in the belt pouch with the tin. For knife and tools, I selected a partially serrated Spyderco folding wallet knife, which is substantial for its size. It can even be used to split a branch by hammering it through with a small log. I didn't mention this knife in Chapter 7 because it is a discontinued item. A survival wire saw was also chosen, as were a couple of razor-knife blades.

For medical situations, a packet of triple antibiotic ointment and four lengths of medical tape applied to a thin piece of plastic, ready to pull off and use, were included. Multi-purpose items included aluminum foil, sewing thread and needles, a Fresnel magnifier and tick tweezers. For miscellaneous items, a pencil and three sheets of waterproof paper (removed from a pad) were added. Also included were small laminated instructions for the water-purification tablets and for fishing knots.

For a small survival kit, this is pretty complete. The only thing missing is parachute cord, which I normally carry in various other places (remember my hat). If you don't, you might want to add it to the kit.

Small Kit #2 in Large Tin & Belt Pouch

This small kit is also in a tin but is much larger than the previous kits. It is held in a belt pouch with supplemental items in various outer compartments of the pouch. This is a main advantage of a combination – tin and pouch – kit. Although the tin holds all the smaller items, the components in the outer compartments are readily available for use. Let's examine it a little closer.

I started with a large tin that measures 6-1/2 inches long x 3-5/8 inches wide x 2-1/2 inches high and quickly realized that its size would allow it to be used as a large cup or cook pot. I wanted a way to hold it over a fire so I made a bail to fit the pot from a piece of antenna off a car. I drilled holes on each side of the tin so the bail could be inserted. The tin could now be hung over a fire for cooking, or the bail could be removed and duct-taped inside the lid.

The pouch measures 7 inches high x 4 inches wide. The back zippered compartment (where the tin resides) is 2-1/2 inches thick. The front flap pocket is expandable, and with the supplemental items inside, it is about 2 inches thick at the widest point. The front cover has a small Velcro pouch that was perfect for the compass (see below). The pouch can be belt worn or over the shoulder.

For fire and light, I first chose the ToolLogic Survival Light/Fire Knife (see Chapter 7), which provides me with the large flint bar and a section on the knife to strike it. A waterproof match case with 20 strike-anywhere waterproof matches was placed in the tin, along with a tub candle, a small BIC lighter and 10 Tinder-Quik Fire Tabs. For a light, I chose a Blast Flashlight (see Chapter 2), which fit in the front flap section of the pouch.

To fulfill the signaling requirement, a Featherweight signal mirror and Skyblazer whistle were selected (see Chapter 3) and placed in the tin. A Brunton Classic orienteering compass was picked for its size, as it fit perfectly in the small front Velcro pocket.

The food and water requirement was satisfied with a complete bottle of Potable Aqua water-purification tablets, a small water bag, a fishing kit (containing 10 #8 hooks, six #6 hooks, eight split shot and four small snap swivels), 50 feet of 20-lb. line and two bouillon cubes. All of these items were added to the tin. Because there was still room available in the tin, I also added an Esbit folding pocket stove with four solid-fuel tablets inside.

The shelter and protection components were a survival blanket, an emergency poncho and SPF-20 lip balm, all added to the tin. Parachute cord and emergency sunglasses were added to the front flap pocket.

Knives and tools included the survival fire knife mentioned above, which also went into the front flap pouch. A survival wire saw was included inside the tin.

For medical, I used one of the small waterproof pouch kits described in Chapter 8. It includes two adhesive

Small Kit #1's belt pouch and its contents.

bandages, two butterfly closures, one 2x2-inch sterile gauze pad, one packet of triple antibiotic ointment, four Extra Strength Tylenol, two antacid tablets, two antiseptic towelettes and two alcohol prep pads. This mini medical kit was placed in the front flap pouch.

Multi-purpose items included a Fresnel magnifier, 2 feet of aluminum foil, snare wire and dental floss rewound on a sewing bobbin. Items for the miscellaneous section included sewing needles, six safety pins (three different sizes) and several cut-down sheets of waterproof paper and a small pencil.

This concludes Small Kit #2. As you can see, although the overall size has increased only slightly, the number and size of the components increased dramatically. In this kit, we have a full-size folding knife, a full-size orienteering compass, a full-size flashlight, parachute cord, a folding pocket stove to cook on and a large-enough tin to cook in. Again, these are the advantages of combining a tin and a pouch when assembling a survival kit.

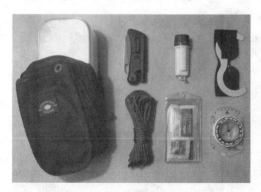
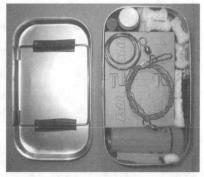

Small Kit #2. The belt pouch with tin in the back zippered section is shown at left. The items to the right are placed in the front flap section, or Velcro pocket. The right photo shows the tin open with contents. The wire bail can be seen taped inside the lid.

All the contents of the large tin as described in the text for Small Kit #2.

Small Kit #3 in Palletized Pouch

The last small kit we will make uses an OR Organizer Pouch, which has three foldout pallets as the container. This pouch has two belt loops on the back to be worn on a belt and two small nylon loops on the top so you can attach a shoulder strap.

Fire and light needs were again met with the ToolLogic Survival Light/Fire Knife with the large flint stick and striker. I chose the Mini-Mag Solitaire flashlight, with one extra battery, which could slide into the flint compartment on the knife (see Chapter 7). A large BIC lighter, a tub candle, a full waterproof container of Lifeboat matches (see Chapter 2) and eight Tinder-Quik Fire Tabs were also added.

The capability to signal came with a StarFlash signal mirror. A full-size Suunto Leader M-3DL orienteering compass was selected for navigation purposes.

Water and food included a full bottle of Potable Aqua water-purification tablets, two water bags, a fishing kit (14 assorted hooks, six swivels, six split shot and one fly spinner), 50 feet of fishing line and one survival fishing Yo-Yo (see Chapter 5).

For shelter and protection, an emergency poncho and survival blanket were selected, along with 30 feet of parachute cord and a lip balm. I already identified the knife selected and added a wire survival saw.

The medical selection was four bandages, one knuckle bandage, one finger bandage, two 2x2-inch gauze pads, medical tape (re-rolled on a thin piece of plastic sheet), four butterfly bandages, two packets of triple antibiotic ointment, one sting

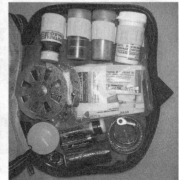

The OR pouch closed, open showing folded pallets and with the end net pouch open.

Here, the entire kit is open with the pallets unfolded. Note how most of the items have their own section in one of the pallets. Loops in the top of the net section on right hold round items secure, with the remaining items secured with the net cover when the pallets are folded and the case is zipped.

relief pad, four alcohol prep pads, two antiseptic towelettes and four Extra Strength Tylenol tablets. It was all placed into a small zip-lock bag.

For multi-purpose devices in this kit, I chose a bandana and a small roll of duct tape. Miscellaneous items included a 3-foot drinking tube, two zip-lock bags, one small garbage bag and two large garbage bags. Several small and medium cable ties, laminated instructions for the water-purification tablets and fishing knots, toilet paper, sewing needles, eight safety pins, sewing thread, dental floss, waxed string and a small thermometer were also added.

Kit #3 is a very complete kit, utilizing a tremendous amount of items chosen for their size and shape as well as their fulfilling a required category. And before we leave this kit, let's go back a moment to thinking outside the box and talk about adaptability. Let's say you want to go for an extended hike and want to take this kit with you. But you want to also carry water. Of course, you could carry a canteen slung over your shoulder. However, if you want one easy-to-carry package, why don't we take the Gregory hydration unit with shoulder straps that we saw in Chapter 5? It just so happens that Kit #3 fits perfectly in the back outside pouch of this hydration unit. Now you have a complete survival kit and 110 fluid ounces of water, and it can all be carried

Combining Small Kit #3 with the Gregory hydration unit is a perfect solution for a long hike. The Gregory unit was chosen because Kit #3 fit perfectly in the outside pouch.

like a small pack. It also provides additional bungee cords to attach a small sweater or jacket.

So far we have used some type of belt pouch as the container for the small kits. Many people today are wearing small fanny packs, so before leaving this section, let's build a small survival kit in a fanny pack.

Small Kit #4 in Fanny Pack

For fire and light, I selected a Doan Magnesium/Flint Bar with striker, a Blast flashlight, 10 Tinder-Quik Fire Tabs, a Pink Lady candle and 20 waterproof strike-anywhere matches in a waterproof match case.

For signaling, a Featherweight signal mirror and a Skyblazer whistle were chosen. For navigation, the Brunton Classic orienteering compass was given the nod.

Food and water requirements were met with Potable Aqua, a 2-gallon water bag, a fishing kit, fishing line and two power bars. Shelter and protection included a survival blanket, an emergency poncho, emergency sunglasses, parachute cord and lip balm.

For a knife, I changed to a Victorinox Hunter, which has a good size saw, so the wire survival saw was left out. Medical components were the same as those in Small Kit #2.

Multi-purpose items included a Fresnel magnifier, a small roll of duct tape and aluminum foil. Miscellaneous items consisted of sewing needles and safety pins.

When all was said and done, there was still enough room in the small fanny pack for additional items, but since we covered each component section, you could add whatever additional items you needed or wanted.

As you can see, once you get familiar with the individual component sections, you can quickly go through each to select the item(s) you desire.

The mini and small kits built in this chapter are only examples to illustrate the selection process and the size of these kits. There are many other configurations you could use in designing your own kit, but you should now at least understand the basics. Depending on need and space limitations, components can be switched from one kit to another, such as the ToolLogic Survival Light/Fire Knife and a wire survival saw being traded for a Victorinox Hunter, which already has a substantial saw in it.

The contents of Small Kit #4 and the finished product.

CHAPTER 13
MAKING MEDIUM AND LARGE KITS

Medium and large survival kits only differ from mini and small kits in size. The component groups remain the same, but we begin to use larger items, or more items, from each group. A medium to large kit should also sustain an individual for a longer period of time than a mini or small kit. You should have more adequate equipment, some emergency food or rations, and a drinkable water supply.

All of the medium and large kits include water, except the first one, due to the configuration of the container, which is an adventure vest.

MAKING MEDIUM KITS

Medium Kit #1 in an Adventure Vest

I chose as my container a Cabela's Safari vest, as it provided the arrangement of pockets I desired and was a relatively inexpensive ($49.95) quality product. It has 16 various pockets and several "D" rings for securely attaching items.

I have looked at various survival vests over the years and they all seemed to have the same problem. After components were selected and tucked away in various pockets, the items would proceed to fall to the bottom of the pockets. The finished product looked like a vest with bulging pockets and did not hang properly from the person wearing it. I set out to rectify this problem.

My initial thought was that the items being placed in various pockets should be palletized or packaged in a way that the individual segments would fill their designated pocket. In this manner, the pockets would remain flat, and the items would not fall to the bottom of the pocket. Some components would be specifically selected for their size and shape. The results of the planning, picking and packaging is a survival vest that only weighs 7 pounds complete and that provides all the required components for a medium-size kit. Let's look at the components selected (keeping in mind that some were selected specifically for the container) and then examine how they were packaged.

For fire and light, a ToolLogic Survival Light/Fire Knife was selected, as it also had the flint included. A Mini-Match was also selected for the magnesium bar and as a back-up flint. A box of Storm wind-proof/waterproof matches was chosen because I knew they would be placed in a waterproof envelope, and they are flatter than the round containers (something preplanned). For tinder, six Tinder-Quik Fire Tabs were included, and for a flashlight, a Blast Light was chosen.

The signaling components were a StarFlash Signal Mirror, as it fit perfectly in a small pocket on the front of the vest, and a Skyblazer whistle. For navigation, a good quality Suunto MSDL Leader orienteering compass was chosen.

I wanted to increase the water and food group, because a medium-size kit must sustain an individual for a longer period. I selected the 2-gallon water bag for its size when folded because it completely filled a front pocket, keeping the pocket square. Emergency rations were two M.R.E. (see Chapter 5) entrées, as they fit

MAKING MEDIUM KITS

This adventure vest from Cabela's proved to be a perfect container for Medium Kit #1.

perfectly in the inside pockets, one on each side. For water purification, a complete bottle of Potable Aqua was added. A fishing kit included 50 feet of 12-lb. fishing line, two 12-inch, 20-lb. stainless-steel wound leaders, two #8 snelled hooks, eight #8 hooks, 10 #5 hooks, 10 split shot, six snap swivels, one large hook for use as a gaff, a Daredevle spoon and one razor prep blade. As you can see, more fishing tackle is added in a medium kit, anticipating a longer duration in the field. This section was completed with snare wire and two aluminum loaf pans, folded as described earlier.

For shelter and protection, I specifically wanted a heavy-duty Space All-Weather Blanket, as it affords both protection and a tarp. When folded, this blanket/tarp fit perfectly in the rear pocket of the vest without any sagging. A bug head net was included along with a poncho and lip balm.

In regard to parachute cord, I wanted as much as was practical, but the problem with parachute cord is packaging. If it is rolled, it will normally fall together and end up in the bottom of a pocket. I had a front pocket of the vest already chosen for this cord, but I wanted it to fit so the pocket would remain flat. I took a piece of flat plastic and cut it 5-1/2 inches wide x 6-1/2 inches high. I then cut in 1/4 inch on each side, 1/4 inch from each end. This provided a pallet on which to wind the parachute cord. The pallet took two complete windings, providing a total of 65 feet of cord. When the pallet is placed inside the front pocket, the pocket retains its shape as planned. The knife selection was discussed earlier, and to supplement the tools, a wire survival saw was added. Medical was again completed using the Mini-Med kit I make.

Multi-purpose items included two large contractor bags because one of each, after folding, fit perfectly in each inside pocket along with the M.R.E. entrée. A small roll of duct tape, a Fresnel magnifier, 3 feet of aluminum foil, 2-gallon-size zip-lock bags and four small zip-lock bags were also added. The miscellaneous items included laminated survival cards, a roll of toilet paper, a compressed sponge (for collecting dew) and assorted needles and safety pins.

Some of the individual components were placed in waterproof pouches selected for the size pocket in which they would be inserted. The components were selected for size and configuration of each individual pouch instead of keeping them in a specific component group. Certain items were placed in separate pockets that did

The left photo contains the waterproof pouch used as a component container for the front top-left pocket. The pouch is turned upright for insertion. The second pouch down is for the front bottom-right pocket, and below that is the plastic pallet for the parachute cord. The completed vest (with no bulges) is shown in the other two photos.

not have a pouch. The compass and survival cards, for instance, were inserted in a pocket above and behind the water bag.

As you can see from the accompanying photos, the adventure-vest project was a success. The vest does not have any bulges nor is it misshapen. For a complete medium-size survival kit, it is easily stored (possibly folded in the rear of your vehicle or trunk) and ready to wear for any hike or adventure. To supplement this kit with water, you could carry a canteen on a belt or with a shoulder strap. If you desire a Nalgene bottle or a bottle of spring water from a store, Campmor sells a bottle carrier that is adjustable for various bottles and provides a carry strap for your shoulder.

Medium Kit #2 in Shoulder Bag

Using a container that can be hand carried or slung over a shoulder, this kit uses a shoulder bag manufactured by Franklin Covey (this particular bag is from their Government Products Group). Called a Sport Bag, it is water-resistant (not waterproof) and provides various multi-functional (we like that) pockets and zippered pouches. It has both a shoulder strap and a top carry handle and measures 7-1/2 inches wide x 8-1/2 inches high by approximately 6 inches deep (depending on how heavily it is stuffed).

For fire and light, I chose a Mini-Match magnesium/flint bar with striker, which was attached to a zipper pull of an inside compartment. A waterproof vial of Lifeboat matches was included with a large BIC lighter and 10 Tinder-Quik Fire Tabs. A Blast flashlight was also selected, as it fit nicely in a specific sectional divider. It was secured to an attachment ring over the divider.

The signaling group was represented by a StarFlash Signal Mirror, which fit in a credit card slot inside the bag, and a Fox 40 whistle, which was clipped to a "D" ring on the outside of the bag with a mini snap link. For navigation, a Suunto A-10

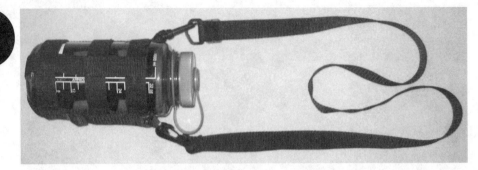

The Campmor bottle carrier for a supplemental water supply.

orienteering compass was used because it is shorter than some and fit the rounded lid pouch section on the front of the bag.

Water and food was increased with a 1-quart military canteen full of water. I found two plastic tubes with screw-on caps that, when taped bottom-to-bottom, were the same height as the canteen. In one of these tubes, I placed five granola bars, and in the other one, I placed coffee bags with sugar. I selected a small titanium cup with folding handles because it fit over the plastic tubes perfectly. The above items all fit in a rear compartment on the bag. An Esbit folding pocket stove with four fuel tabs was included as well as one Mainstay 2400-calorie Emergency Food Ration. This section was topped off with some hard candy, two aluminum loaf pans folded as previously described, a small water bag, a bottle of Potable Aqua water-purification tablets and snare wire.

For shelter and protection, an Ultralite Poncho/Tarp (see Chapter 6) was selected because it fit in the front flap pouch like it was made for it. An emergency poncho was added in the event the poncho/tarp was used as a tarp. A survival blanket, emergency sunglasses and parachute cord were also included.

A Gerber E-Z-Out folding knife, with partially serrated blade, was selected for a knife, as it is substantial and it clipped nicely into the section alongside the Blast flashlight. A wire saw was packaged in an old 35 mm camera lens filter holder and fit in the other side of the rounded section of the front flap, where the compass was stored. For medical, again the Mini-Med kit was used.

Multi-purpose items included a flat sponge, a Fresnel magnifier and a small roll of duct tape. Miscellaneous items were aluminum foil, a pen and pencil with four sheets of waterproof paper, two hand warmers, a titanium Spork (a

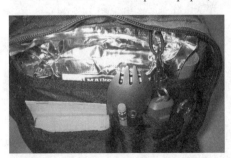

The back and front inside pallets of the front section are shown here. Note how items have been placed in individual slots and pockets. Mini-Match hangs on left of right photo.

combination spoon-fork) made by Snow Peak, a plastic tube and a survival/ medical handbook.

For the size, this is a very complete kit. It has the food, water, tools and equipment needed to sustain life in an emergency situation for at least a couple of days.

As you can see, with this type of a container, you can place different components in various sections so they can be easily found. While this always adds size to the container, it also adds to the kit's convenience. Again, trade-offs are part of the game.

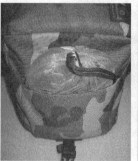

Additional components of Medium Kit #2: The Ultralite Poncho in the front flap pocket; the compass and survival saw that reside in the pocket of the flap that covers the poncho; and the canteen, titanium cup and tubes that hold the food bars on one end and the coffee and sugar on the other end, which all fit in the rear compartment.

Medium Kit #3 in Fanny Pack

A fanny pack is handy, as it can be worn around your waist, can carry water, and as long as you don't make it too heavy, you can pretty much forget it's there. It can also allow you to be properly prepared for an emergency situation. The fanny pack used for this kit measures approximately 12 inches long x 6 inches wide x 7 inches high, with bottle holders on each end. I placed a 16-ounce Nalgene water bottle in each holder, providing a total of 32 ounces of available water.

This fanny pack kit has 16-ounce water bottles on each end.

The signaling and navigation components for Medium Kit #3 are shown packaged in a zip-lock bag in the left photo. The right photo has the fire and light components at top left, the first-aid kit at top right and the SOG SEAL Revolver (a combination knife and saw) at the bottom. These component packages were placed in the front pouch of the fanny pack.

Because of the configuration of the container (a large open rear section and smaller front section), some of the components were packaged together to prevent smaller items from finding their way to the bottom of the bag.

For fire and light, I started with a Princeton Tec Attitude with 3 ultra-bright LEDs that runs 150 hours on four AAA batteries. A waterproof vial of Lifeboat matches, a Doan magnesium fire starter and a pink lady candle were included for fire, along with a waterproof match case filled with cotton balls soaked with petroleum jelly. I topped off this component section with two small green Lightsticks, and everything was packaged in a clear front pouch.

The signaling and navigation sections were combined in a small zip-lock bag that included a StarFlash Signal Mirror, a Skyblazer whistle and a Suunto Woodsman A-30-L orienteering compass.

I have already addressed the water bottles for the water and food section. A Frontier filter and a bottle of Potable Aqua were added for water purification. A titanium Sierra cup with folding handle was included, along with a fishing kit and line. Food included one M.R.E., three granola bars, two tea bags, four sugar packets and two bouillon packets; all (excluding the M.R.E.) were placed in a small zip-lock bag.

Shelter and protection started with a heavy-duty Space All Weather Blanket/ Tarp. An emergency poncho and sunglasses were added along with lip balm, a package of anti-bacterial wipes and parachute cord. A waterproof pouch with extra socks and underwear were also included.

The knife and tool section was filled with a SOG SEAL Revolver (as you will recall from Chapter 7, this is a fixed-blade knife with a blade on one end and a saw on the other) and a U-Dig-It folding trowel.

For medical needs, I included a small medical kit in a red clear-sided pouch (as seen in Chapter 8). Multi-purpose items included zip-lock bags in various sizes and garbage bags, a Fresnel magnifier, duct tape, aluminum foil and a bandana.

Miscellaneous items consisted of toilet paper, sewing needles and safety pins.

All the small components were placed in an old small candy tin so, again, they would not fall to the bottom of the bag, making them difficult to locate. This tin included the Potable Aqua, fishing kit and line, lip balm, Fresnel magnifier,

Here are the components that were placed in the rear compartment of the fanny pack.

duct tape, aluminum foil, sewing needles and safety pins. The small tin was held closed with electrical tape and placed in the rear section with all the remaining components.

Again, the above medium-size kit is complete in its component requirements. It provides for a comfortable way to carry your survival kit as well as a supply of water and emergency rations.

Medium Kit #4 in Waterproof Case

This next kit is more suitable for someone involved in water-borne operations, such as canoeing. It is actually a re-make kit, in that almost all the components are taken directly from an earlier kit (Medium Kit #3). As you have already learned, items are often selected for the size and shape of the container. In this instance, upon transferring the components from Medium Kit #3 to Medium Kit #4, a few modifications took place in order to accommodate the changed shape.

First, we start with a Pelican waterproof case measuring 13 inches long x 10-1/4 inches wide x 6 inches high. It has an "O"-ring seal with a purge valve, which makes it an ideal container for water operations.

Upon examining the components from Medium Kit #3, I determined that the two 16-ounce Nalgene water bottles could be traded for one 32-ounce bottle. The larger bottle fit perfectly in the side of the Pelican case, with an Alpine stainless-steel cup on the bottom (you will recall from Chapter 5 that the Alpine cup fits over the bottom of a 32-ounce Nalgene bottle). Therefore, the original titanium Sierra cup was replaced with the Alpine cup to accommodate the different size. Because of the configuration of the container, an Esbit folding pocket stove with four fuel tablets was also able to fit inside. Because this kit was mainly for water operations, consideration was given to additional signaling. Room was available, so two Skyblazer XLT Flares and an emergency strobe were added as well.

MAKING LARGE KITS

The selected waterproof case for Medium Kit #4.

MAKING LARGE KITS

Making large survival kits is not difficult, especially if you stick to the component list. The difference is the anticipated duration of the survival situation. You want to think longer term and add additional items such as clothes and more emergency food. The basics never change!

Large Kit #1 in Backpack

This first large kit will be built as a modular unit. The main pack will contain all required components. Additional and supplemental pouches, with further shelter and protection for longer duration, can then be attached onto the main pack. In this manner, the main pack will always complete the survival mission, while the additional components will make a survival situation more comfortable.

I started with a Camelbak H.A.W.G., which is a small pack developed for military, highly mobile, short-range recon missions. It is a hydration pack (which means it has a water bladder with drinking tube), and even though I don't normally prefer this type of pack, it is the first I have seen with a zippered back-access panel for the bladder. This means you don't have to take everything out of the pack to get a filled bladder back in (which is the normal way and the reason why I usually don't like bladders). The bladder holds 3 liters (about 100 ounces) of water and so you start out with over 3 quarts or three 32-ounce Nalgene bottles or military canteens. Additionally, the pack has two compartments with a total of 1100 cubic inches of cargo-carrying space.

A civilian-type pack, such as a North Face or Kelty, would also suffice, but they normally have one large cargo carrying area. As discussed earlier, this makes it difficult to locate your equipment. Also, civilian-style packs are not normally as durable as packs made for the military. However, military packs tend to be heavier and the trade-off is durability vs. weight.

The Camelbak H.A.W.G. also has MOLLE attachment points for additional pouches, which I wanted to add to the rear of the pack to further segregate individual component groups. I purchased five small MOLLE pouches from

 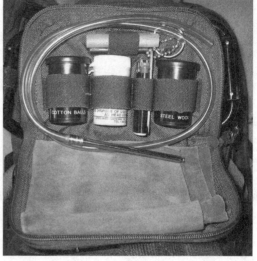

The back of the Camelbak H.A.W.G. pack with the fire-kit pouch (at the top) and the five smaller pouches attached (two in the middle and three at the bottom). The right photo shows the contents of the fire-starting pouch.

Blackhawk that connected to the attachment points on the back of the pack and provided me with just the type of storage I desired. I also used another medium-size pouch for a fire-starting kit (which was an old pen-gun-flare pouch made by London Bridge, a company who makes special operations equipment). I attached this pouch to the top of the rear of the pack, above the other pouches. I now could separate small component groups and have easy access to them without having to enter the pack.

Keep in mind, that unlike minimalist and ultra-light backpackers, I wanted durability and a sectional container. I understand that more compartments increase the weight, but this was a trade-off I was willing to make.

On each kit so far, we have gone through each component section individually before indicating where those components went. Because of the divisional sections available, and due to the amount of equipment that will be placed in this kit, the placement and packaging of components will be discussed as we go. No component section is left out, so let's get packing.

The top fire-starting pouch was filled with a container of cotton balls with petroleum jelly, a vial of Lifeboat matches, a small BIC lighter, a container of steel wool, a magnesium/flint rod and a striker. I also added some Tinder-Quik Fire Tabs in an inside pouch for good measure, as well as a blowing tube (the one discussed in Chapter 11 with the telescoping antenna tube). An 8-1/2 x 10-1/2-inch piece of leather was also added, for transferring an ember to a nest, and was folded to fit the pouch. This provided a lot of fire-making components, but as we have learned, fire is critical to survival.

The top-left MOLLE pouch was equipped with a spare bulb for the Princeton Tec Blast flashlight, which was hung off a "D" ring on one of the front shoulder straps. This pouch also held a Petzl Tikka Plus headlamp.

The top-right pouch was for cordage. I included a good length of parachute cord and 50 feet of Kelty Triptease Lightline. Although not as versatile or strong as parachute cord, I can store twice as much in the same space. It is highly reflective, with 188-lb. breaking strength, and is good for lashing or tarp lines. I still had parachute cord for all the positive reasons we learned in Chapter 6.

The bottom-left pouch was for water purification. It holds a bottle of Potable Aqua and a bottle of P.A. Plus neutralizer, along with a Frontier filter (for immediate gratification) and two folded loaf pans. The center-bottom pouch holds the small fishing tackle case as described in Chapter 5, along with a set of laminated fishing-knot cards.

The right pouch holds a waterproof case with nine spare AAA batteries and another waterproof pouch with a small repair kit. This repair kit holds a glue stick, a mini sewing awl (as described in Chapter 9), duct and electrical tape, sewing thread and needles, and snare wire.

The five small MOLLE pouches are essentially attached to the cover of a medium-size compartment on the back of the pack. This compartment had a sectional divider and sewed-in organizer sections, so it was utilized for other smaller items and rain gear. The rear section was used to hold a small zippered pouch filled with a waterproof pad, several pens (with lighted tips) and pencils, a soft tailor's tape measure (something I always carry because I'm always designing) and a clear compass protractor. This section also held my small first-aid pouch and work gloves. Several feet of heavy-duty aluminum foil folded and placed in a zip-lock bag also slid nicely down in the rear section.

In the front sewed-in organizer sections, I placed a Princeton Tec Attitude flashlight, a Victorinox Hunter, a titanium fork and spoon, a stream thermometer, as well as some personally preferred items. A zippered pouch was found that could be inserted perfectly inside the outer compartment, in front of the sewed-in sections. A Marmot light-weight rain jacket and trousers set was placed in the main section of this pouch. An outside zippered section on this pouch held a light-weight skullcap, balaclava, and gloves, made from polypropylene, as well as a large military handkerchief. This pouch slid down in the outer compartment, holding the items in the sewed-in sections firmly.

A small pouch containing a Brunton orienteering compass and a StarFlash signal mirror was placed on one of the front shoulder straps. A Fox 40 whistle was attached to a "D" ring on the side of the pack, and a set of pace beads was attached to a "D" ring on a front shoulder strap. This completed the signaling and navigation requirements.

The large rear compartment was next. I folded a SPACE Emergency Hooded Blanket/Poncho so it would lie against the entire back of the rear compartment, giving additional padding between the contents and my back. In the bottom-left section of the rear compartment, I placed a small, 6 feet x 8 feet Campmor Ultralite tarp, which fit in a small net bag measuring 7 inches long x 4-1/2 inches wide x 2 inches thick. On the right bottom, a Patagonia PuffBall insulated vest (which packs down incredibly small) was placed in a pouch measuring 7 inches long x 5 inches wide x 2-1/2 inches thick. On top of the vest went a mini pot set that I made up. It consists of a small titanium pot and kettle. A Snow Peak titanium auto-start cartridge stove and a small canister of gas (45-minute run time) was placed inside the kettle. This was for a quick cup of tea while a real fire was being made. A wind screen for the stove was placed inside the pot. A bail wire was made for the kettle and placed inside the bottom of a stuff sack, which was cut down to accommodate the size of the set. The resulting package measures 5 inches in diameter x 3-1/2 inches high.

 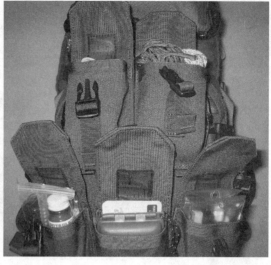

The five component groups, as discussed in the text, shown separately and then inserted in their respective pouches on the backpack.

A small flat stuff sack was used to hold three M.R.E.s and four granola bars. This was placed to the left of the pot set, over the Ultralite tarp. A small supplemental food container made from an old military decontamination kit, which is waterproof, measures 4-1/4 inches high x 2-7/8 inches wide x 1-7/8 inches thick. A small tin containing four teabags and eight sugar packets, sealed with electrical tape, was placed in the container. Another small tin with various hard candies was also inserted. There was room alongside the tins to slide three packages of the Emer'gen-C energy drink, and on top, four bullion cubes and small salt-and-pepper shakers fit quite nicely. The entire container fit on top of the pot set.

I also wanted a Polartec long-sleeve shirt, and it fit in a zippered pouch 8 inches long x 6 inches wide x 2-1/2 inches thick that just fit above the other items. A medium-size waterproof envelope held an extra pair of socks and underwear and slid down alongside the emergency blanket in the back.

A small toiletry kit – a plastic container holding a small tube of concentrated soap, a small tube of toothpaste and a collapsible toothbrush – fit inside the top of the pack, which was an empty semi-rounded section. I re-wound some dental floss on a small plastic stick that then slid into a clear plastic tube with a cover. A Featherweight signal mirror slid down into the container and kept everything from rattling (as well as providing a backup signal mirror). The container, because of its rounded shape, fit nicely in the top of the pack. The addition of a mini pack towel and package of moist field towelettes completed the inside of the pack.

A SPEC-OPS Brand Frontal Assault Pouch, measuring 7-1/2 inches long x 5 inches wide at the top and 3-1/2 inches wide at the bottom x 1 inch thick, was attached to the top of the left-front shoulder strap. It was used to hold a toilet kit containing toilet paper, small zip-lock bags and small antibacterial wipes. A container of bug repellant and two granola bars were also added.

This finishes the basic pack, which now is a very complete large survival kit. However, in order to last longer in a survival situation, we should add some

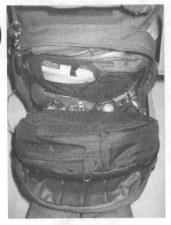

The outer compartment open with the rain-gear bag inserted and the rear section holding the first-aid kit, notebook, work gloves and individual items in the sewed-in sections.

additional clothes and shelter. I obtained two pouches, measuring 15 inches long x 5 inches wide x 4 inches high, that will mount under the compression straps on the side of the pack, one on each side. In one pouch, a Byer Moskito hammock was added. This is a very lightweight hammock, with a complete sewn-in bug net (like a jungle hammock), that packs in a very small package. A

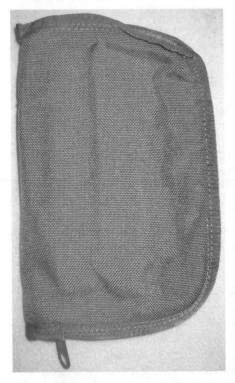

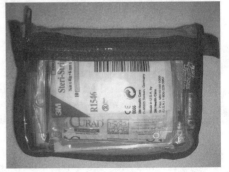

The notebook closed and open, and the first-aid kit.

Clockwise starting at left: The components of the back compartment shown in the configuration in which they are placed within the pack; the mini pot set packaged; the mini pot set open, showing its contents; the toiletry kit open; and the closed toiletry kit.

large Campmor Ultralite Tarp, measuring 10 feet x 12 feet, was included in this pouch with extra parachute cord.

The second pouch holds a pair of adventure trousers with zip-off legs (which also provides a pair of shorts), a light-weight, long-sleeve adventure shirt, and a set of light-weight, quick-dry long underwear.

On the bottom of the pack, a SnugPak Jungle sleeping bag was attached with additional straps. This sleeping bag only weighs 25 ounces and packs into its own stuff sack that measures 6 inches long x 4-3/4 inches in diameter. It even has a rollaway mosquito net that zips into the hood to cover your face. This

The completed large kit in a pack, with extended duration packages added. The Blast flashlight can be seen hanging on the right shoulder strap with the pace beads. The large pouch for the toilet kit and bug repellant can be seen at the top of the left shoulder, with the small pouch for the compass and signal mirror under that pouch.

The AR-7 Air Force Survival Rifle, which is now manufactured by Henry. The bottom-left photo shows the rifle disassembled, while the bottom-right photo shows all the components stored in stock.

was for the convenience section. Two large and two small carabiners were also attached to the outside of the pack.

The finished kit at this point only has a medium folding knife. Keep in mind that I always carry my fixed-blade leg knife, as discussed in Chapter 7. If you don't carry a fixed-blade knife on your belt or elsewhere, consider adding one to the large kit.

This concludes the first large survival kit. As you can see, a large kit can take some time to design and build, but it is not complicated. All you have to do is stick with the component selection process, ensuring that no group is left out. Redundancy is fine, especially for some groups.

I won't put you through the entire process for another large kit, but let's further discuss kits of this size. If you wanted a large kit for a water-borne operation, everything in the above pack could be re-packaged into a water bag. The medium size with the horizontal zipper would work well. All the smaller components packaged in the small pouches on the back of the pack could be placed in another container and placed in the bag. Double-bag all component groups and all clothing in zip-lock bags. There should be some additional room in the bag, and therefore, you could add a strobe light, some flares and even a survival rifle.

The Henry Survival Rifle, which packs into a flotation stock, is ideal for water-borne operations such as canoeing and rafting. This is a new version of the original Air Force AR-7 survival rifle. It is a 22-caliber semi-automatic rifle that breaks down easily. All the components can be packed into the stock, which floats. I haven't played with one of these new ones, but I have an original AR-7, which was made by Armalite. Although it is only a 22, it is good for obtaining food (small animals). Of course, this survival rifle isn't limited to water-borne operations. It could be strapped to a pack or kept in a vehicle, aircraft or ATV.

The container for a large kit really depends on how the kit will be carried. As you will see in the next chapter, large kits can be packed in a large carry bag if it will stay in a vehicle or aircraft. Of course, if you plan on carrying it, you should consider something with shoulder straps, such as the pack discussed above.

Environmental conditions should be mentioned again. If in a snow area, extra items like snowshoes and a snow shovel should be considered, as well as extra warm clothes. A snow-melting stove like we saw in Chapter 5 might also be contemplated. If you are going to be in an area where water is plentiful, freeze-dried meals might be the best food choice. If you are in an arid environment, like a desert, M.R.E.s might make more sense, as they don't need water to be eaten.

Large survival kits are just expanded mini-, small- and medium-size kits. Again, THE BASICS NEVER CHANGE! All component groups are used and you keep expanding as the kit grows. Most of the vehicle kits are of the larger size, so as a continuation of large kits, let's move on to the next chapter, Making Vehicle Kits.

MAKING LARGE KITS

CHAPTER 14

MAKING VEHICLE KITS

There are many types of vehicle survival kits. They can be broken down into the type of vehicle being used, the activity being performed and the environment in which the activity is being conducted. Of course, we always know the type of vehicle for which the kit is being made. We normally know the activity we plan on performing, such as driving a car into the backcountry, taking a truck off-road, fishing with a boat, whitewater rafting or maybe flying for fun. However, we cannot always be certain of the environment; therefore, we need to plan for the worst so we don't have to hope for the best.

Vehicle kits will be broken down into the following categories for ease of discussion:

+ **Automobile Survival Kits**
+ **Truck Survival Kits**
+ **Boat Survival Kits**
+ **Aircraft Survival Kits**
+ **Snowmobile Survival Kits**
+ **ATV Survival Kits**

Each type of vehicle kit should include items or equipment that will not only provide you with the personal survival items you need (which should be in your personal survival kit and carried in the vehicle) but also those necessary to fix or repair the type of vehicle you are using, to supplement your personal items, and to provide additional equipment for the specific activity in which you are involved. And because you are using a vehicle, you can carry larger items, or more items, than with a personal kit.

Obviously, your personal survival kit is the basis of your survival. Although you should always carry at least a mini kit on your person, a small, medium or large kit can be left in a car or truck. Even an aircraft and larger boats should have a designated survival kit. But when you get into smaller modes of transportation such as canoes, kayaks, snowmobiles or ATVs, you will need to remember to include one of your survival kits as the personal survival component of the overall kit.

Spare parts really depend on the vehicle being used. I will not provide an individual list of parts that should be carried for each designated vehicle discussed in this chapter. Some specific items may be covered, however, if they are something that every vehicle of that type might use.

You should also keep in mind that a vehicle can also provide various emergency survival items itself. Most cars and trucks have a rearview or side mirror, which can be broken off in an emergency and used as a signal mirror. Vehicles are full of wires that can be used for lashing, and seating material and carpets can be used for protection and insulation from the cold. The list could

An example of survival gear for a regular car. All these items are described in the text.

go on and on, but always examine what you have (thinking outside the box) and determine how it might be used for something other than for which it was originally intended.

AUTOMOBILE SURVIVAL KITS

As mentioned above, you should have a personal survival kit that goes with you when you get out of the vehicle. You should also have equipment that can be used to repair your vehicle. This should include a spare tire, jack and lug wrench in the event you get a flat tire. Additional tools for minor repairs should also be considered, such as screwdrivers, pliers, a hammer and hacksaw. Jumper cables, a tow cable or strap, tire chains (if in an extremely snowy area), and possibly some small replacement parts such as fan belts and radiator hoses should be carried. A shovel can be extremely useful in many situations, and a small ax or saw can assist in removing a tree across the road.

Safety items should always be maintained in your vehicle. These items would include flares, a reflective safety vest, heavy work gloves and a brightly colored flag to hang off your side mirror to warn of an emergency situation.

For personal survival, a container of water (as large a container as is practical, or several smaller bottles) should be carried. Keep in mind that if you are in an area where the temperature goes down below freezing, you should carry the water in a metal canteen or other type of container that can be placed over a fire or stove to melt the water (or melt snow into water).

Some extra food, rain gear, a first-aid kit, some survival blankets, a regular blanket and some duct tape are also items that should be included. In cold regions, you should also carry extra clothing. If you normally wear dress shoes for work, a pair of hiking shoes or boots should be kept in your vehicle. If you have to leave your vehicle and walk, you won't want to be wearing dress shoes. In the winter, I carry a pair of winter boots, especially when I'm working in a suit and tie with dress shoes. I also carry a winter parka, as a dress trench coat only goes so far in a blizzard.

For emergency communications, you should have a cell phone. At one time, vehicle cell phones were permanently mounted in the vehicle, and, of course, those are still available. I recommend having a handheld portable, however. If you have to leave the vehicle, the phone can go with you. The same is true for CB radios. There are vehicle-mounted units, but you can get handheld units that can be used in or out of the vehicle. Multipurpose is always the way to go.

If room is available, there are some additional items that could prove useful. These could include a 12-volt emergency power supply, a power inverter, a portable compressor, a small survival stove, and a metal cup or pot to boil water, cook food or melt snow for water.

Of course, the size of your vehicle limits the amount of equipment and supplies that you can carry. However, with a little innovative effort, you will be surprised at how much stuff you can store in a small amount of space. Remember to select items that will serve more than one purpose, reducing the size of the overall package.

TRUCK SURVIVAL KITS

When I speak of trucks, I'm talking about personal transportation vehicles, such as pickups and SUVs. Some pickups and SUVs are four-wheel drive, and if you go off-road, you need even more equipment than if you stay on normal roads.

Obviously, trucks have more room than automobiles, which means your equipment can be stored in a larger bag or container, or you can segregate items

The minimal equipment maintained in the author's truck, as detailed in the text.

Here is the equipment maintained in the large black bag, as well as a close-up of the 12-volt power unit with jumper cables and the 2.5-gallon water container.

into containers of various sizes. Some trucks have room to build a container, such as a box, in the back or behind the seat to contain your survival gear.

The first thing you need to include is your personal survival kit. I recommend a medium or large kit for a truck, especially if you go off-road. All the items discussed for automobiles would also be appropriate for a truck kit. However, with the additional room, you can increase the amount of food and water, as well as some additional equipment to assist in getting un-stuck (again, especially for those going off road).

Some handy items for a truck are a tow strap, some recovery straps, a portable come-along (also known as a power puller), D-Shackles, snatch-block pulleys and some heavy work gloves. If your vehicle is high, you also might consider a High-Lift jack. Another nice but expensive (especially if you don't do a lot of off roading) piece of equipment is a permanent winch mounted on the truck.

I try to keep the same supplies in my truck at all times, adding special items as needed for specific trips. I keep a bag that carries a blanket, some rope, two M.R.E.s, a 32-ounce Nalgene bottle with an Alpine cup on the bottom, an Esbit stove with four fuel tablets, a Sierra survival stove (see Chapter 5), duct tape, parachute cord, a SOG Seal pup knife, a radio with a wind charger, a small compressor, work gloves, five light sticks, a poncho and three large contractor bags.

I have a flashlight mounted to the dash of my truck and a fire extinguisher mounted to the center console. A rescue tool for cutting the seat belt and breaking the window is mounted to the headliner between the two front seats so either the driver or passenger can reach it.

A 12-volt power unit with jumper cables and an AC-voltage regulator and flashlight are also part of my normal equipment, along with a 2.5-gallon water container. This container is nice, as it is half the size of most heavy-duty water containers, making it easier to carry. The only place I've seen it available is from Brigade Quartermasters.

Additional equipment includes a small bag with rain gear, hat and gloves. The Medium Survival Kit #2 in a shoulder bag now lives in my truck. I also keep a folding shovel (and a collapsible snow shovel in the winter), a hatchet, a large Becker BK-9 knife (see Chapter 7), a Sawvivor saw and a tool kit. These are my tools for various emergency chores. I also have a tow strap, some D-Shackles and a come-along. A large first-aid kit is always present as are a roll of duct tape, some flares and an emergency vest and flag. When driving in the backcountry, I also carry my M-6 survival rifle (see Chapter 12) with built-in survival kit.

BOAT SURVIVAL KITS

The type and/or size of boat will dictate what type of boat kit is required. For the purpose of this discussion, we are mainly concerning ourselves with smaller boats such as canoes, kayaks, inflatables and small fishing boats used for freshwater adventures.

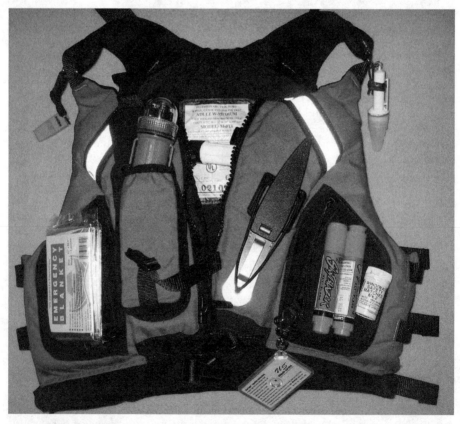

The author's PFD, which is equipped with a whistle, survival blanket, a strobe, knife, flashlight, two signal flares, lifeboat matches and a survival mirror.

BOAT SURVIVAL KITS

Here is a boat kit for a canoe. At top left is Medium Kit #4 in a waterproof case. Below that is a collapsible pail for bailing and below that a pack towel. At top center is the PFD above a throw bag, all-weather blanket, duct tape, tube tent and large fishing kit. At top right is a SealLine waterproof portage pack that contains emergency rations, extra clothes and other equipment. The fishing kit and survival rifle (shown below the pack) also go into the pack. Finally, on bottom is a spare paddle.

Keeping in mind that you are on water with a boat kit, there is equipment essential to this type of transportation. First, your personal survival kit should be in a waterproof container. If you want to carry a kit that is not normally waterproof, then either place it in a waterproof container or double-bag it in freezer bags, placing the first one upside down in the second.

You should carry an additional waterproof bag or container with an extra set of clothes and a towel. There is a very light-weight towel called a "pack towel" that can be packed down very small. Emergency rations should also be a part of this additional container.

Your next piece of gear should be a PFD (Personal Flotation Device). Try to get one with several pockets that either zip or have Velcro fasteners. Include emergency devices in these pockets such as a strobe, signal mirror and signal flares. I have "D" rings on mine and attach a survival whistle to one of them on the outside. Also add a fire-starter kit, a survival blanket and a flashlight. A quality knife in a sheath should be attached to the outside. If there is room, add some energy bars. The idea is that if you fall overboard and lose your other equipment (I'm not talking about the ocean here, but freshwater) you should have on you the essentials to survive. Fire starting is important because you want to get warm and dry as quickly as possible.

For the boat itself, you should have an extra paddle (tied inside the boat), a throw bag (for tossing to a person overboard) and something with which to bail water, or a small bilge pump. A roll of duct tape is also a good idea, as it can be used to help repair the boat as well as a broken paddle.

All gear and equipment placed in the boat should be secured by tying it down. If the boat is capsized, you don't want your stuff floating downstream, or worse, sinking.

If you are on a wilderness trip, you might consider a weapon. The Henry Survival Rifle discussed at the end of Chapter 13 would be a good choice, as the entire rifle is stored in a floating stock, making it ideal for water-borne operations. A larger fishing kit would also be a good choice since you are already on water, and catching fish would be a readily available source of food.

AIRCRAFT SURVIVAL KITS

A survival kit for an aircraft should be able to accommodate the amount of people on the aircraft. An individual kit is not required for each person, but the total equipment available should be able to provide for everyone. Of

A possible aircraft survival kit for two people. At top left is the Air Force survival rifle. Below that is a folding shovel, chainsaw in a can, multi-purpose tool, military folding knife and BK-9 fixed-blade knife. A mini-hacksaw and vise-grip pliers are below the can. Below that are two emergency sleeping bags, a 2-gallon water bag, two survival blankets, two all-weather blankets with hoods and two tube tents. To the right is a heavy-duty carry bag with shoulder strap. Below the bag are four emergency rations, 16 water rations, two head nets, two emergency sunglasses, a 32-ounce Nalgene bottle with Alpine cup, a first-aid kit, a survival manual, two rolls of toilet paper, bug repellant, two emergency ponchos and a sewing kit. The equipment shown at bottom left will be described under the next photo.

AIRCRAFT SURVIVAL KITS

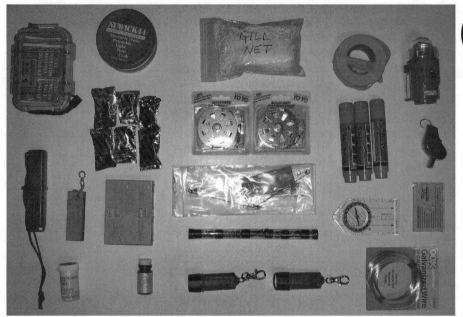

A close-up view of the bottom-left section of the aircraft survival kit shown in the previous photo. The small waterproof box at the top left holds tea bags, sugar and bouillon packets. Next is a Nuwick 44-hour candle with six WetFire tinders below it. At left is a Strike Force Fire Starter, a Doan Magnesium Block, an Esbit pocket stove with fuel and a vial of Lifeboat matches, which complete the fire section. A bottle of Potable Aqua completes the water-purification section. The fishing section, in the middle, provides a gill net, two survival Yo-Yos, a SpeedHook and a tackle kit. Below that are two Blast flashlights. The right side shows flagging tape, a strobe light, three flares, a whistle and a signal mirror. There is an orienteering compass for navigating, and a roll of snare wire completes the food section.

course, if you are flying, you will have a personal survival kit with you. But you can't count on everyone else being as prudently equipped.

All survival gear, excluding your personal kit, should be stored in either a large pack or carry bag that can be readily transported away from the aircraft in the event that is necessary, such as the threat of fire or explosion.

At least one good fire-starting kit should be incorporated with the minimum of a magnesium fire starter, waterproof/wind-proof matches, a lighter, some candles, and fire starters such as cotton balls saturated in petroleum jelly or Tinder-Quik Fire Tabs. A good quality waterproof flashlight with extra batteries should be available for at least every other person.

There should be a supply of drinking water and emergency food and rations, again, for the amount of people present. Include bouillon cubes, tea or coffee bags, and sugar. A stove, such as an Esbit pocket stove, and cooking utensils should also be included, with at least one cup for each person. Include several water bags for storage, as well as a means to purify water.

In addition to emergency sleeping bags (or real sleeping bags if room is available) and parachute cord, tube tents or other emergency shelters should be available for everyone on board.

A good-sized, fixed-blade survival knife, a machete or ax should be included in the kit along with a folding saw, a survival saw and multi-purpose tool. Some additional repair tools to include are a hacksaw, vise-grip pliers and a good quantity of duct tape.

A first-aid kit that can handle the number of people present and any severe injuries that may result from a crash landing should be part of the package. This kit should also include lip balm, sunscreen, insect repellent and a head net for each person.

Signaling devices should include at least one signal mirror, survival whistle, signal flares, strobe light, and a signal panel or flagging tape. If there is room available, at least a couple whistles and signal mirrors would be better. A good quality orienteering compass should be included for navigation.

For food collection, include a freshwater fishing kit, some SpeedHooks (see Chapter 5), several survival Yo-Yos, a gill net and some commercial snares or snare wire.

Finally, include some aluminum foil, toilet paper, a sewing kit and a survival manual. If a weapon is desired, the Henry Survival Rifle (former AR-7 Air Force Survival Rifle discussed in chapter 13) would be ideal.

SNOWMOBILE SURVIVAL KITS

I've talked to numerous people who drive snowmobiles and it never ceases to amaze me how many don't carry a survival kit. Although they travel at relatively high speeds over various terrain for 10 or more miles, very few carry a survival kit. I ask what happens if they break down 10 miles out in the woods, and they respond that they never really thought about it. This is when a survival kit is important. To build a serviceable snowmobile kit, a personal survival kit, such as a good small or medium kit, would be your starting point, adding items as indicted below.

Of course, you should have repair items to keep your machine going if it breaks down. This would include basic repair parts and tools, extra gas and oil, and a towrope if you are out with more than one machine.

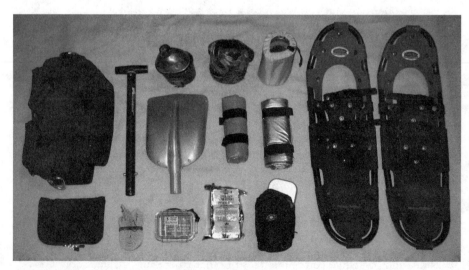

Here is a minimal survival kit, as described in the text, for a snowmobile.

If you are snowmobiling, you are out in cold conditions, so you should have a survival kit that will help you survive that environment. A rack of some type on your snowmobile may be handy to accommodate additional gear. Extra warm clothes are important, especially if you have to spend a night in the wilderness. To protect you from the elements, include shelter options, such as a tube tent or light-weight tarp. If room allows, a small one-man tent would also be a great advantage. A survival sleeping bag would be a minimum; a small sleeping bag would be better.

A small stove is needed to melt snow into drinking water, and some emergency rations are needed to keep your energy level up in the cold. Snowshoes and a collapsible snow shovel should be attached somewhere to your snowmobile. If you end up having to walk out, you will be glad you have the snowshoes.

ATV SURVIVAL KITS

ATVs are similar to snowmobiles, as they are often used as recreational vehicles. Although ATVs are taken out into the wilderness, I often get the same response from owners questioned about survival kits: "What survival kit?"

A survival kit for an ATV should be similar to that for a snowmobile. Repair parts and tools, extra gas and oil, and a towrope are musts. If you don't have a winch on the machine, you might consider a small come-along to get yourself out of a sticky situation. There are many types of ATV racks that provide extra storage space for carrying gear.

You still need a good personal kit, with additions to the shelter and emergency food or rations section. Unless you take your ATV out in the snow, you should trade the snow shovel for a folding shovel, and leave out the snowshoes.

Additional clothing should depend on the environment and season. Carry extra water and something in which to cook in addition to a first-aid kit. Don't take a chance. If you break down and have to spend a night in the wilderness, be prepared.

Summary Of Vehicle Kits

While there are some similarities between the different vehicle survival kits, there is gear that is specific to the type of vehicle being used. Always remember to keep the environment, number of people and weather conditions in mind when venturing out. Some gear will provide for all of these factors, while some items must be specifically chosen to serve in certain circumstances.

Vehicle kits are not difficult to make. Plan for the worst, and be prepared to survive!

CHAPTER 15

IN CONCLUSION

The previous chapters have provided you with all the basics for building your own survival kits. I hope it has been fun as well as informative. Making your kit results in a finished product that reflects YOUR needs. You no longer have to depend on well-intentioned, but often deficient, commercial kits. By making your own kit, you have the flexibility to choose the type and size of container, and by packing it yourself, you know the exact location of each item.

Keep the basics in mind when you build a kit. Be sure the items you choose allow you to build a fire, signal, gather water and food, navigate, construct a shelter and carry out basic first aid.

In order for you to have an easy way to ensure you fulfill each component section, the following table will help remind you that each section must have at least one item. It will also help you remember what items you have placed in what kits. Photocopy this table and fill in those components you have chosen for your kit. You will quickly notice if anything has been left out.

Remember the four P's: Plan-It, Pick-It, Pay-For-It and Pack-It. Plan what you want your kit to be before getting started, and know what you want it to accomplish. Pick the appropriate components to fulfill your goals. Determine your budget at the beginning, so you don't allocate too many funds to specific items and end up not having enough left to complete your kit. Pack your kit so the finished product provides for the desired results.

Seasonal and environmental factors should also be considered before you begin. Don't just hope a kit will provide for the season or environment in which you end up; plan for it!

Understanding the purpose of the components, we should now know how to choose the correct size components for making the smallest, yet serviceable, survival kit possible. We know that the smaller the survival kit we build, the better chance we will carry it.

One of my goals in writing this book was to make survival kits interesting and easy to build. Hopefully, I have accomplished that and you have gained an insight into the uncomplicated process of designing and building your own kit. I want you to be motivated because you will never regret the effort. I want you to be innovative and experiment with new ideas and items. Share your ideas with friends, as nobody has the ideal kit. They can always be better, smaller, more waterproof, etc. When it comes to survival kits, there are no experts. We can all learn new techniques or a different way to package something. The important thing is to make a kit!

There are some important issues that we have not addressed in this book. First, there are various components in a survival kit that expire or go bad, such as medicine, food, iodine tablets, etc. For this reason, we must check our kits periodically. I have always set a schedule where I check each of my survival kits each New Year. The New Year is always a holiday anyway, and it gives me an opportunity to review the components for expiration. In this manner, I know that all of my kits are good for the coming year. Of course, whatever system works for you is best. But check them before you need them.

Lastly, never (and I mean never) take or borrow items from your survival kit. Your kit is for emergencies only. When you need it, you need all of it. If you find that there are certain items in your kit that you need or use during non-emergency times, then buy extra. It is well worth the extra money. When you are thrust into a survival situation, and your kit is fully intact, you will be glad you have not raided it prematurely.

SURVIVAL KIT COMPONENT SELECTION	
Date:	**Kit Name or Description:**
Fire & Light:	
Signaling:	
Water & Food:	
Shelter & Protection:	
Knives & Tools:	
Medical:	
Multi-Purpose Items:	
Miscellaneous:	

APPENDIX I

RECOMMENDED SURVIVAL KITS

Mini / Small Kits

KIT SIZE: Mini Kit
CONTAINER: Waterproof Pouch

MINI KITS

FIRE & LIGHT:
1. Mini-Match Magnesium Firestarter with striker
2. Half a book of matches (waterproofed with Thompson's Water Seal) and striker
3. Two Tinder-Quick Fire Tabs
4. Photon Micro-Light II

SIGNALING:
1. Aluminum foil (can be used for a signal mirror)

NAVIGATION:
1. 20mm button compass

WATER & FOOD:
1. Mini water bag
2. Aluminum foil can be used to make a cup to boil water for purification
3. Fishing kit w/ six hooks, four swivels and six split shot
4. 30 feet fishing line wound on a floss bobbin
5. Snare wire
6. One bouillon packet

SHELTER & PROTECTION:
1. None in kit (a survival blanket, emergency poncho and parachute cord can be carried on your person)

KNIVES & TOOLS:
1. Swiss Army Knife with two blades

MEDICAL:
1. Packet triple antibiotic ointment
2. Two butterfly closures
3. Alcohol prep pads

MULTI-PURPOSE:
1. Aluminum foil
2. Fresnel magnifier

MISCELLANEOUS:
1. Two safety pins
2. Two needles (magnetized)

KIT SIZE: Mini Kit
CONTAINER: Aluminum Foil

FIRE & LIGHT:
1. Mini-Match Magnesium Firestarter with striker
2. Half a book of matches (waterproofed with Thompson's Water Seal) with striker
3. Cotton balls w/petroleum jelly (wrapped in Saran Wrap)

SIGNALING:
1. Aluminum foil container can be used for a signal mirror

NAVIGATION:
1. 20mm button compass

WATER & FOOD:
1. Aluminum foil can be used to make a cup to boil water for purification
2. Fishing tackle kit w/ 2 hooks, 2 swivels and 4 split shot
3. One fishing leader (can also be used as a snare)
4. 30 feet of fishing line wound on a floss bobbin
5. Snare wire

SHELTER & PROTECTION:
1. None in kit (a survival blanket, emergency poncho and parachute cord can be carried on your person)

KNIVES & TOOLS:
1. Swiss Army knife with one blade, small scissors, a small file, tweezers and toothpick

MEDICAL:
1. One packet triple antibiotic ointment
2. Two butterfly closures
3. Two alcohol prep pads

MULTI-PURPOSE:
1. Aluminum foil
2. Fresnel magnifier

MISCELLANEOUS:
1. Two safety pins
2. Two needles (magnetized)

KIT SIZE: Mini Kit
CONTAINER: Altoids Tin

FIRE & LIGHT:
1. Mini-Match Magnesium Firestarter with striker
2. Six waterproof/windproof lifeboat matches
3. Five Tinder-Quick Fire Tabs
4. Fresnel magnifier
5. Candle (cut down to fit tin)
6. Photon Micro-Light II flashlight

SIGNALING:
1. Custom-made signal mirror

NAVIGATION:
1. Button compass

WATER & FOOD:
1. Mini water bag
2. Two feet aluminum foil
3. 20 Potable Aqua tablets repackaged in mini glass vial
4. Fishing tackle kit w/ 12 assorted hooks, 6 swivels and 6 split shot
5. 20 feet fishing line wound on sewing bobbin
6. Snare wire

SHELTER & PROTECTION:
1. Survival blanket and parachute cord carried on person (nothing in tin)

KNIVES & TOOLS:
1. Survival wire saw
2. Two razor knife blades

MEDICAL:
1. One packet triple antibiotic ointment
2. Two butterfly closures

MULTI-PURPOSE:
1. Nylon string
2. Glue stick

MISCELLANEOUS:
1. Laminated instructions for Potable Aqua
2. Laminated fishing knots guide

KIT SIZE: Mini Kit
CONTAINER: Bamboo Pole

FIRE & LIGHT:
1. Mini-Match Magnesium Firestarter with small saber saw blade for a striker
2. Cotton balls w/ petroleum jelly (wrapped in Saran Wrap)
3. Mini-Mag AAA Solitaire flashlight

SIGNALING:
1. None (recommend carrying a whistle on key ring or aluminum foil for a signal mirror in pocket)

NAVIGATION:
1. 20mm button compass

WATER & FOOD:
1. Small glass vial w/ 20 Potable Aqua water-purification tablets
2. Non-lubricated condom (for use as a water bag)
3. Fishing tackle kit w/ eight #8 hooks, two #6 hooks, four swivels and six split shot
4. 40 feet fishing line wound on a sewing bobbin

SHELTER & PROTECTION:
1. Parachute cord wrapped on handle (a survival blanket or emergency poncho can be carried on your person)

KNIVES & TOOLS:
1. Christy survival knife
2. Saber saw blade

MEDICAL:
1. None (although duct tape wound on flashlight can be used as a wound closure)

MULTI-PURPOSE:
1. None

MISCELLANEOUS:
1. None

KIT SIZE: Mini Kit
CONTAINER: Plastic Cigar Case

FIRE & LIGHT:
1. Mini-Match Magnesium Firestarter with striker
2. Half book of matches (waterproofed with Thompson's Water Seal) and striker
3. Cotton balls w/ petroleum jelly (wrapped in Saran Wrap)

SIGNALING:
1. Aluminum foil (can be used for a signal mirror)

NAVIGATION:
1. 20mm button compass

WATER & FOOD:
1. Aluminum foil can be used to make a cup to boil water for purification
2. Fishing kit w/ two hooks, two swivels and four split shot
3. Fishing leader (can also be used as a snare)
4. 30 feet fishing line wound on a floss bobbin
5. Snare wire
6. Packet chicken bouillon

SHELTER & PROTECTION:
1. None in kit (a survival blanket, emergency poncho and parachute cord can be carried on your person)

KNIVES & TOOLS:
1. Swiss Army Knife with one blade, small scissors, a small file, tweezers and toothpick

MEDICAL:
1. Packet of triple antibiotic ointment
2. Butterfly closures
3. Alcohol prep pads

MULTI-PURPOSE:
1. Aluminum foil
2. Fresnel magnifier

MISCELLANEOUS:
1. Two safety pins
2. Two needles (magnetized)

KIT SIZE: Mini Kit
CONTAINER: M-6 Scout Survival Rifle

FIRE & LIGHT:
1. Mini-Match Magnesium Firestarter with small saber saw blade for a striker

SIGNALING:
1. Aluminum foil can be used for signal mirror

NAVIGATION:
1. None, although a small compass can be carried on your person

WATER & FOOD:
1. Small glass vial w/ 20 Potable Aqua water-purification tablets
2. Aluminum foil can be used as a container to purify water
3. Fishing kit w/ eight #8 hooks, two #6 hooks, four swivels and six split shot
4. 20 feet fishing line wound on a sewing bobbin

SHELTER & PROTECTION:
1. Parachute cord wrapped on barrels of rifle
2. Survival rifle w/ eight .410 rounds and 34 .22 long rifle rounds
3. An emergency blanket and poncho can be carried on your person

KNIVES & TOOLS:
1. CRKT MDP Stiff Kiss knife
2. Survival wire saw

MEDICAL:
1. None

MULTI-PURPOSE:
1. Aluminum foil

MISCELLANEOUS:
1. None

KIT SIZE: Small Kit #1
CONTAINER: Small Tin & Belt Pouch

FIRE & LIGHT:
1. Mini-Match Magnesium Firestarter with striker
2. 12 Lifeboat waterproof/ windproof matches (in a small zip-lock bag rolled and taped)
3. Small BIC lighter
4. Tub candle
5. Six Tinder-Quick Fire Tabs
6. CMG Infinity LED Task Light

SIGNALING:
1. StarFlash signal mirror

NAVIGATION:
1. Fixed-dial compass

WATER & FOOD:
1. Small glass vial w/ 20 Potable Aqua water-purification tablets
2. Small glass vial w/ 20 P.A. Plus neutralizer tablets
3. Small water bag
4. Fishing kit w/ 10 #8 hooks, six #6 hooks, four swivels and eight split shot
5. 50 feet fishing line wound on sewing bobbin
6. Aluminum foil
7. Snare wire
8. The tin used as a container for a cooking pot

SHELTER & PROTECTION:
1. Survival blanket
2. Emergency poncho

KNIVES & TOOLS:
1. Spyderco folding wallet knife
2. Survival wire saw
3. Two razor-knife blades

MEDICAL:
1. Packet of triple antibiotic ointment
2. Four lengths of medical tape (applied to a thin piece of plastic, ready to pull off and use)

MULTI-PURPOSE:
1. Fresnel magnifier
2. Aluminum foil
3. Sewing thread
4. Sewing needles
5. Tick tweezers

MISCELLANEOUS:
1. Pencil
2. Three sheets waterproof paper
3. Laminated instructions for water-purification tablets
4. Laminated instructions for fishing knots

KIT SIZE: Small Kit #2
CONTAINER: Large Tin & Belt Pouch

FIRE & LIGHT:
1. Flint bar in ToolLogic Survival Fire Knife
2. Waterproof match case w/ 20 Strike Anywhere matches
3. Tub candle
4. BIC lighter
5. 10 Tinder-Quick Fire Tabs
6. Blast flashlight

SIGNALING:
1. Featherweight signal mirror
2. Skyblazer signal whistle

NAVIGATION:
1. Brunton classic orienteering compass

WATER & FOOD:
1. Bottle of Potable Aqua water-purification tablets
2. Small water bag
3. Fishing kit w/ 10 #8 hooks, six #6 hooks, four swivels and eight split shot
4. 50 feet fishing line wound on sewing bobbin
5. Two bouillon cubes
6. Esbit folding pocket stove w/ four solid fuel tablets
7. The tin used as a container for a cooking pot

SHELTER & PROTECTION:
1. Survival blanket
2. Emergency poncho
3. SPF-20 lip balm
4. Parachute cord
5. Emergency sunglasses

KNIVES & TOOLS:
1. ToolLogic Survival Fire Knife
2. Survival wire saw

MEDICAL:
1. Two adhesive bandages
2. Two butterfly closures
3. 2-inch x 2-inch sterile gauze pad
4. Packet triple antibiotic ointment
5. Four Extra-Strength Tylenol
6. Two antacid tablets
7. Two antiseptic towelettes
8. Two alcohol prep pads

MULTI-PURPOSE:
1. Fresnel magnifier
2. Two feet aluminum foil
3. Snare wire
4. Dental floss rewound on a sewing bobbin

MISCELLANEOUS:
1. Sewing needles
2. Six safety pins
3. Several cut-down pieces of waterproof paper
4. Small pencil

KIT SIZE: Small Kit #4
CONTAINER: Fanny Pack

FIRE & LIGHT:
1. Doan magnesium/flint bar w/striker
2. 20 waterproof Strike Anywhere matches in a waterproof match case
3. Pink Lady candle
4. 10 Tinder-Quick Fire Tabs
5. Blast flashlight

SIGNALING:
1. Featherweight signal mirror
2. Skyblazer whistle

NAVIGATION:
1. Brunton Classic orienteering compass

WATER & FOOD:
1. Bottle of Potable Aqua water-purification tablets
2. 2-gallon water bag
3. Fishing kit w/ 14 hooks, six swivels, six split shot and one fly spinner
4. 50 feet fishing line wound on sewing bobbin
5. Two Power Bars

SHELTER & PROTECTION:
1. Survival blanket
2. Emergency poncho
3. Lip balm
4. Parachute cord
5. Emergency sunglasses

KNIVES & TOOLS:
1. Victorinox Hunter knife
2. Survival wire saw

MEDICAL:
1. Four adhesive bandages
2. Four butterfly closures
3. Two 2-inch x 2-inch sterile gauze pads
4. One knuckle bandage
5. One finger bandage
6. Two packets triple antibiotic ointment
7. Medical tape re-rolled on a thin plastic sheet
8. One sting-relief pad
9. Four Extra-Strength Tylenol
10. Two antiseptic towelettes
11. Four alcohol prep pads

MULTI-PURPOSE:
1. Fresnel magnifier
2. Small roll of duct tape
3. Aluminum foil

MISCELLANEOUS:
1. Sewing needles
2. Eight safety pins

MEDIUM KITS / LARGE KITS

Recommended Survival Kits

MEDIUM /LARGE KITS

KIT SIZE: Medium Kit #1
CONTAINER: Adventure Vest

FIRE & LIGHT:
1. ToolLogic Survival Fire Knife w/ flint and striker
2. Mini-Match Magnesium/Flint Bar w/ striker
3. Box of Storm waterproof/ windproof matches
4. Six Tinder-Quick Fire Tabs
5. Blast flashlight

SIGNALING:
1. StarFlash signal mirror
2. Skyblazer signal whistle

NAVIGATION:
1. Suunto MSDL Leader orienteering compass

WATER & FOOD:
1. Two-gallon water bag
2. Two MRE entrées
3. Bottle of Potable Aqua water-purification tablets
4. Fishing kit w/ two 20-lb leaders, #8 snelled hooks, eight #8 hooks, 10 #5 hooks, 10 split shot, six snap swivels, one large hook (gaff), a Daredevle spoon and one razor prep blade
5. 50 feet of 12-lb fishing line
6. Two aluminum loaf pans folded flat
7. Snare wire

SHELTER & PROTECTION:
1. Heavy-duty Space All Weather Blanket
2. Bug headnet
3. Emergency poncho
4. Lip balm
5. 65 feet parachute cord wrapped on a custom pallet made to fit in front pocket of vest

KNIVES & TOOLS:
1. ToolLogic Survival Fire Knife w/ flint and striker
2. Survival wire saw

MEDICAL:
1. Two adhesive bandages and two butterfly closures
2. One 2-inch x 2-inch sterile gauze pad
3. One packet triple antibiotic ointment
4. Four Extra-Strength Tylenol
5. Two antacid tablets
6. Two antiseptic towelettes and two alcohol prep pads

MULTI-PURPOSE:
1. Two large contractor bags
2. One small roll of duct tape
3. Fresnel magnifier
4. Three feet aluminum foil
5. Two-gallon Zip-Lock bags
6. Four small Zip-Lock bags

MISCELLANEOUS:
1. Laminated survival cards
2. Roll of toilet paper
3. Compressed sponge
4. Several needles
5. Several safety pins

68

KIT SIZE: Medium Kit #2
CONTAINER: Shoulder Bag

FIRE & LIGHT:
1. Mini-Match Magnesium Firestarter with striker
2. Waterproof vial of waterproof/windproof Lifeboat matches
3. BIC lighter
4. 10 Tinder-Quick Fire Tabs
5. Blast flashlight

SIGNALING:
1. StarFlash signal mirror
2. Fox 40 signal whistle

NAVIGATION:
1. Suunto A-10 orienteering compass

WATER & FOOD:
1. One-quart military canteen
2. Five granola bars
3. Six coffee bags w/ sugar
4. Esbit folding pocket stove w/ four solid fuel tablets
5. One Mainstay 2400-calorie emergency food ration
6. Hard candy
7. Bottle of Potable Aqua water-purification tablets
8. Small water bag
9. Titanium cup
10. Two aluminum loaf pans folded flat
11. Snare wire

SHELTER & PROTECTION:
1. Ultralight poncho/tarp
2. Survival blanket
3. Parachute cord
4. Emergency sunglasses

KNIVES & TOOLS:
1. Gerber E-Z-Out folding knife
2. Survival wire saw

MEDICAL:
1. Two adhesive bandages and two butterfly closures
2. 2-inch x 2-inch sterile gauze pad
3. Packet of triple antibiotic ointment
4. Four Extra-Strength Tylenol
5. Two antacid tablets
6. Two antiseptic towelettes and two alcohol prep pads

MULTI-PURPOSE:
1. Flat sponge
2. Fresnel magnifier
3. Small roll of duct tape

MISCELLANEOUS:
1. Aluminum foil
2. Four sheets of waterproof paper w/ pencil
3. Two chemical hand warmers
4. Titanium spork
5. Plastic tube
6. Survival/medical handbook

KIT SIZE: Medium Kit #3
CONTAINER: Fanny Pack

FIRE & LIGHT:
1. Doan magnesium fire starter with striker
2. Waterproof vial of waterproof/windproof Lifeboat matches
3. Waterproof match case filled w/ cotton balls soaked in petroleum jelly
4. Pink Lady candle
5. Two small light sticks
6. Princeton Tec Attitude LED flashlight

SIGNALING:
1. StarFlash signal mirror
2. Skyblazer signal whistle

NAVIGATION:
1. Suunto Woodsman A-30-L orienteering compass

WATER & FOOD:
1. Two 16-oz Nalgene water bottles
2. Frontier water filter
3. Bottle of Potable Aqua water-purification tablets
4. Titanium Sierra cup
5. Fishing kit w/ fishing line
6. Three granola bars
7. One MRE entrée
8. Two tea bags w/ four sugar packets
9. Two bouillon packets

SHELTER & PROTECTION:
1. Heavy-duty Space All Weather Blanket
2. Emergency poncho
3. Parachute cord
4. Emergency sunglasses
5. Lip balm
6. Package of anti-bacterial wipes
7. Waterproof pouch w/ extra socks and underwear

KNIVES & TOOLS:
1. SOG Seal Revolver knife/saw
2. U-Dig-It folding trowel

MEDICAL:
1. Small first-aid kit

MULTI-PURPOSE:
1. Various sized Zip-Lock bags
2. Fresnel magnifier
3. Small roll of duct tape
4. Aluminum foil
5. Bandana

MISCELLANEOUS:
1. Toilet paper
2. Sewing needles
3. Safety pins

KIT SIZE: Medium Kit #4
CONTAINER: Waterproof Case

FIRE & LIGHT:
1. Doan magnesium fire starter with striker
2. Waterproof vial of waterproof/ windproof Lifeboat matches
3. Waterproof match case filled w/ cotton balls soaked in petroleum jelly
4. Pink Lady candle
5. Two small light sticks
6. Princeton Tec Attitude LED flashlight

SIGNALING:
1. StarFlash signal mirror
2. Skyblazer signal whistle
3. Two Skyblazer XLT signal flares
4. Emergency strobe

NAVIGATION:
1. Suunto Woodsman A-30-L orienteering compass

WATER & FOOD:
1. 32-oz Nalgene water bottle
2. Frontier water filter
3. Bottle of Potable Aqua water-purification tablets
4. Alpine stainless steel cup
5. Esbit folding pocket stove w/ four fuel tablets
6. Fishing kit w/ fishing line
7. Three granola bars
8. One MRE entrée
9. Two tea bags w/ four sugar packets
10. Two bouillon packets

SHELTER & PROTECTION:
1. Heavy-duty Space All Weather Blanket
2. Emergency poncho
3. Parachute cord
4. Emergency sunglasses
5. Lip balm
6. Package of anti-bacterial wipes
7. Waterproof pouch w/ extra socks and underwear

KNIVES & TOOLS:
1. SOG Seal Revolver knife/saw
2. U-Dig-It folding trowel

MEDICAL:
1. Small first-aid kit

MULTI-PURPOSE:
1. Various sized Zip-Lock bags
2. Fresnel magnifier
3. Small roll of duct tape
4. Aluminum foil
5. Bandana

MISCELLANEOUS:
1. Toilet paper
2. Sewing needles
3. Safety pins

KIT SIZE: Large Kit #1
CONTAINER: Backpack

FIRE & LIGHT:
1. Magnesium fire starter with striker
2. Waterproof vial of waterproof/ windproof Lifeboat matches
3. 35mm film canister filled w/ cotton balls soaked in petroleum jelly
4. 35mm film canister filled w/ "0000" steel wool
5. Small BIC lighter
6. Several Tinder-Quik Fire Tabs
7. One blowing tube
8. One 8.5-inch x 10.5-inch piece of leather
9. Princeton Tec Blast flashlight
10. Spare bulb for flashlight
11. Princeton Tec Attitude LED flashlight
12. One Petzl Tikka Plus headlamp

SIGNALING:
1. StarFlash signal mirror
2. Fox 40 signal whistle

NAVIGATION:
1. Brunton orienteering compass
2. One set of pace beads

WATER & FOOD:
1. One Frontier water filter
2. Bottle of Potable Aqua water purification tablets
3. Bottle P.A. neutralizing tablets
4. Two folded loaf pans
5. Fishing kit w/ fishing line
6. One small titanium pot
7. One small titanium kettle
8. Snow Peak titanium auto-start cartridge stove
9. Small gas canister for stove
10. Three MRE entrees
11. Four granola bars in pack and two in outside pouch
12. Four tea bags w/ eight sugar packets
13. Small tin of hard candy
14. Three packages of Emer'gen-C energy drink
15. Four bouillon cubes
16. Salt and pepper

SHELTER & PROTECTION:
1. Heavy-duty Space All Weather Blanket w/ hood
2. 6-feet x 8-feet ultralite tarp
3. Patagonia PuffBall insulated vest
4. Polartec long-sleeve shirt
5. Marmot ultra-light breathable rain jacket and trousers
6. Parachute cord
7. 50 feet Kelty Triptease Lightline reflective cordage
8. Work gloves
9. Polypropylene skull cap
10. Polypropylene balaclava
11. Polypropylene gloves
12. Large military handkerchief
13. Emergency sunglasses
14. Bug repellent
15. Package of anti-bacterial wipes
16. One waterproof pouch w/extra socks and underwear

KNIVES & TOOLS:
1. Victorinox Hunter knife
2. Folding Gerber saw

MEDICAL:
1. Small first-aid kit

(CONTINUED on page 172)

LARGE KITS

KIT SIZE: Large Kit #1 (CONTINUED from page 171)
CONTAINER: Backpack

MULTI-PURPOSE:
1. Nine spare AAA batteries
2. Repair kit w/glue stick, mini sewing awl, duct and electrical tape, sewing thread and needles, and snare wire
3. Heavy-duty aluminum foil

MISCELLANEOUS:
1. Small zippered pouch w/ waterproof pad, several pens with lighted tips, pencils, soft tailor's tape measure and clear compass protractor
2. Small toiletry kit w/ tube of concentrated soap, small tube of toothpaste, collapsible toothbrush, dental floss and featherweight signal mirror
3. Mini pack towel
4. Package of moist field towelettes
5. Titanium spoon and fork
6. Stream thermometer
7. Toilet paper
8. Two large carabiners
9. Two small carabiners
10. Sewing needles
11. Safety pins

OPTIONAL SHELTER SIDE POUCH:
1. Byer Moskito hammock
2. 10-feet x 12-feet ultralight tarp
3. Extra parachute cord

OPTIONAL CLOTHING SIDE POUCH:
1. Adventure trousers w/ zip-off legs
2. Lightweight long-sleeve shirt
3. Lightweight quick-dry long underwear

OPTIONAL SLEEPING POUCH:
1. Lightweight SnugPak jungle sleeping bag

Recommended Survival Kits

VEHICLE KITS

KIT SIZE: Vehicle
CONTAINER: Aircraft

VEHICLE KITS

PERSONAL SURVIVAL KIT:
1. Small to medium personal survival kit

FIRE & LIGHT:
1. Extra fire starting kit w/ magnesium fire starter, waterproof/windproof matches, a lighter, some candles and fire starters such as cotton balls with petroleum jelly or Tinder-Quik Fire Tabs (in PFD)
2. Flashlight w/extra batteries

SIGNALING:
1. Signal mirror (several)
2. Emergency strobe
3. Signal flares
4. Survival whistle (several)
5. Signal panel or flagging tape

NAVIGATION:
1. Good orienteering compass

WATER & FOOD:
1. Container of water or several water bottles for each person
2. Extra food and rations for each person
3. Folding pocket stove w/ fuel tabs
4. Metal cup for each person
5. Water purification tablets or device and water bags
6. Complete fishing kit with addition of speed hooks, several survival Yo-Yos and a gill net
7. Commercial snares or snare wire

SHELTER & PROTECTION:
1. Tube tent or other emergency shelter for each person
2. Emergency sleeping bags for each person
3. Parachute cord
4. Lip balm
5. Sunscreen
6. Insect repellent
7. Headnet for each person

KNIVES & TOOLS:
1. Good quality fixed-blade survival knife
2. Machete or ax
3. Folding saw
4. Survival saw
5. Multi-purpose tool
6. Repair tools such as hacksaw and vise-grip pliers

MEDICAL:
1. First-aid kit to handle amount of passengers plus severe injuries that may result from a crash landing

MULTI-PURPOSE:
1. Roll of duct tape
2. Aluminum foil

MISCELLANEOUS:
1. Survival rifle
2. Toilet paper
3. Sewing kit
4. Survival manual

KIT SIZE: Vehicle
CONTAINER: ATV

PERSONAL SURVIVAL KIT:
1. Small to medium personal survival kit

VEHICLE EQUIPMENT:
1. Repair tools
2. Repair parts
3. Extra gas and oil
4. Tow rope

WATER & FOOD:
1. Extra water
2. Emergency food and rations
3. Small stove
4. Cup or pot to melt snow into drinking water

SHELTER & PROTECTION:
1. Tube tent or lightweight tarp
2. Emergency sleeping bag
3. Extra clothes
4. Parachute cord

KNIVES & TOOLS:
1. Folding shovel

FIRST AID:
1. First-aid kit to handle injuries that might occur with an ATV accident

MISCELLANEOUS:
1. Snowshoes

KIT SIZE: Vehicle
CONTAINER: Boat (such as a canoe)

VEHICLE EQUIPMENT:
1. Extra paddle (tied inside craft)
2. Rope throw bag
3. Bailer
4. Bilge pump

VEHICLE SAFETY ITEMS:
1. Personal flotation device (PFD)

PERSONAL SURVIVAL KIT:
1. Waterproof personal survival kit

FIRE & LIGHT:
1. Fire-starting kit w/magnesium fire starter, waterproof/windproof matches, a lighter, some candles, and fire starters such as cotton balls with petroleum jelly or Tinder-Quik Fire Tabs (in PFD)
2. Flashlight in PFD
3. Flashlight in kit

SIGNALING:
1. Signal mirror (in PFD)
2. Emergency strobe (in PFD)
3. Signal flares (in PFD)
4. Survival whistle (in PFD)

WATER & FOOD:
1. Container of water or several water bottles
2. Energy bars (in PFD)
3. Extra food
4. Fishing kit

SHELTER & PROTECTION:
1. Survival blanket (in PFD)
2. Extra clothes in waterproof bag
3. Pack towel

KNIVES & TOOLS:
1. Quality knife (attached to PFD)

MEDICAL:
1. First-aid kit

MULTI-PURPOSE:
1. Roll of duct tape

MISCELLANEOUS:
1. Survival rifle

KIT SIZE: Vehicle
CONTAINER: Automobile

VEHICLE KITS

VEHICLE REPAIR EQUIPMENT:
1. Spare tire
2. Jack
3. Lug wrench
4. Tools for minor repairs
5. Jumper cables
6. Tow cable
7. Tire chains (for extremely snowy areas)
8. Replacement parts

VEHICLE SAFETY ITEMS:
1. Flares
2. Reflective vest
3. Heavy work gloves
4. Brightly colored flag

PERSONAL SURVIVAL KIT:
1. Small to medium size personal survival kit kept in vehicle

EMERGENCY COMMUNICATIONS:
1. Cell phone
2. Portable CB radio

WATER & FOOD:
1. Container of water or several water bottles
2. Extra food

SHELTER & PROTECTION:
1. Rain gear
2. Additional survival blankets
3. Regular blanket
4. Extra clothing
5. Hiking boots
6. Winter parka or heavy trench coat in cold environments

KNIVES & TOOLS:
1. Shovel

MEDICAL:
1. First-aid kit

MULTI-PURPOSE:
1. Roll of duct tape

MISCELLANEOUS:
1. 12-volt emergency power supply
2. Power inverter
3. Portable compressor
4. Small survival stove
5. Metal cup or pot

KIT SIZE: Vehicle
CONTAINER: Snowmobile

PERSONAL SURVIVAL KIT:
1. Small to medium personal survival kit

VEHICLE EQUIPMENT:
1. Repair tools
2. Repair parts
3. Extra gas and oil
4. Tow rope

WATER & FOOD:
1. Emergency rations
2. Small stove
3. Cup or pot to melt snow into drinking water

SHELTER & PROTECTION:
1. Tube tent or other lightweight tarp
2. Small sleeping bag
3. Extra warm clothes
4. Parachute cord
5. Tent (optional)

KNIVES & TOOLS:
1. Collapsible snow shovel

MISCELLANEOUS:
1. Snowshoes

KIT SIZE: Vehicle
CONTAINER: Truck

VEHICLE KITS

VEHICLE REPAIR EQUIPMENT:
1. Spare tire
2. Jack
3. Lug wrench
4. Tools for minor repairs
5. Jumper cables
6. Tow cable
7. Recovery strap
8. Portable come-along
9. D-Shackles
10. Snatch block pulleys
11. Tire chains (in extremely snowy area)
12. Replacement parts
13. High-lift jack (optional)
14. Vehicle-mounted winch

VEHICLE SAFETY ITEMS:
1. Flares
2. Reflective vest
3. Heavy work gloves
4. Brightly colored flag
5. Fire extinguisher
6. Rescue tool

PERSONAL SURVIVAL KIT:
1. Medium to large personal survival kit kept in vehicle

FIRE & LIGHT:
1. Five light sticks
2. Flashlight

EMERGENCY COMMUNICATIONS:
1. Cell Phone
2. Portable CB Radio

WATER & FOOD:
1. 2.5-gallon container of water
2. MREs
3. Extra food
4. Esbit stove w/ fuel tablets or Sierra survival stove

SHELTER & PROTECTION:
1. Rain gear
2. Hat and gloves
3. Additional survival blankets
4. Regular blanket
5. Extra clothing
6. Hiking boots
7. Winter parka or heavy trench coat in cold environment

KNIVES & TOOLS:
1. SOG Seal Pup knife
2. Folding shovel (collapsible snow shovel in winter)
3. Hatchet
4. Large Becker BK-9 knife
5. Sawvivor folding saw

MEDICAL:
1. First-aid kit

MULTI-PURPOSE:
1. Roll of duct tape
2. Parachute cord
3. Rope
4. Three large contractor bags

MISCELLANEOUS:
1. Radio w/ wind charger
2. Five light sticks
3. 12-volt emergency power supply
4. Power inverter
5. Portable compressor
6. Small survival stove
7. Metal cup or pot
8. M-6 Survival Rifle (optional)

APPENDIX II

SUPPLIERS FOR SURVIVAL KIT COMPONENTS

The following is a list of suppliers and manufacturers that sell or make various components that can be used for building a survival kit. They are listed in alphabetical order and some also provide information on specific types of components they offer. If a manufacturer does not sell to the general public, you can contact them for a supplier that handles their product.

ACR Electronics, Inc.
5757 Ravenswood Road,
Fort Lauderdale, FL 33312
Phone: 954-981-3333
Fax: 954-983-5087
www.acrelectronics.com
Manufacturer of safety equipment such as the Firefly Plus Strobe Light.

Adventure Medical Kits
P.O. Box 43309,
Oakland, CA 94624
Phone: 800-324-3517
Fax: 510-261-7419
www.adventuremedicalkits.com
Complete line of adventure medical kits as well as individual medical components.

A.G. Russell Fine Knives
1920 N. 26th Street,
Lowell, AR 72745-8489
Phone: 800-255-9034
Fax: 479-631-8493
www.agrussell.com
Manufacturer and distributor of knives.

AlpineAire Foods
(AKA – TyRy, Inc.)
P.O. Box 1799, Rocklin, CA 95677
Phone: 916-624-6050
Fax: 916-624-1604
www.aa-foods.com
Manufacturer of freeze-dried food.

Backpacker's Pantry
6350 Gunpark Drive,
Boulder, CO 80301
Phone: 303-581-0518
www.backpackerpantry.com
Manufacturer of freeze-dried food.

Becker Knife and Tool Company
See Camillus Cutlery Company.

Blackhawk Industries, Inc.
4850 Brookside Court,
Norfolk, VA 23502
Phone: 800-694-5263
Fax: 888-830-2013
www.blackhawk.com
Manufacturer of nylon tactical gear and HydraStorm hydration systems.

Brigade Quartermasters

1025 Cobb International Drive NW,
Suite 100,
Kennesaw, GA 30152
Phone: 800-338-4327
Fax: 800-892-2999
www.actiongear.com
Survival components, flashlights,
Gill Net, hydration units, knives,
Lifeboat matches, navigation, Otter
boxes, parachute cord, SAS survival
saw, sleeping bags, small pouches,
SpeedHook, tarps, Thompson Snares.

Brownells

200 South Front Street,
Montezuma, Iowa 50171
Phone: 800-741-0015
Fax: 800-264-3068
www.brownells.com
Distributor of firearms-related
products and parts, to include plastic
tubes with end caps.

Browning

One Browning Place,
Morgan, VT 84050
Phone: 800-333-3288
www.browning.com
Manufacturer of firearms,
knives and accessories.

Brunton

620 East Monroe Avenue,
Riverton, WY 82501
Phone: 307-856-6559
Fax: 307-856-1840
www.brunton.com
Manufacturer of Brunton
compasses.

Buck Knives

1900 Weld Blvd.,
El Cajon, CA 92020
Phone: 800-326-2825
www.buckknives.com
Manufacturer of knives.

Busse Combat Knife Company

11651 Country Club Road 12,
Wauseon, OH 43567
Phone: 419-822-6853
Fax: 419-923-2337
www.bussecombat.com
Manufacturer of custom knives.

Byer Manufacturing Company (The)

74 Mill Street, P.O. Box 100,
Orono, ME 04473
Phone: 800-338-0580
www.byeromaine.com
Manufacturer of hammocks.

Cabela's

Phone: 800-237-4444
Fax: 308-254-6745
www.cabelas.com
Manufacturer and distributor
of camping, fishing, shooting
equipment, outdoor clothing, etc.

CamelBak Products, Inc.

1310 Redwood Way,
Suite C, Petaluma, CA 94954
Phone: 800-767-8725
Fax: 707-665-9231
www.camelbak.com
Manufacturer of hands-free
hydration systems.

Camillus Cutlery Company

54 Main Street,
Camillus, NY 13031
Phone: 315-672-8111
Fax: 315-672-8832
www.camillusknives.com
Manufacturer of U.S. Military
approved folding knife,
Air Force pilot survival knife and
owner of Becker Knife and Tools Co.,
manufacturing BK-7 & BK-9
Combat/Utility Knife and the Becker
Patrol Machete.

COMPONENT SUPPLIERS

Campmor

P.O. Box 700,
Saddle River,
NJ 07458
Phone: 800-226-7667
Fax: 800-230-2153
www.campmor.com
Survival components, full line
of camping supplies, Nalgene
bottles, ultralite poncho and
tarps, SealLine water bags.

Cascade Designs, Inc.

4000 1st Avenue South,
Seattle, WA 98134
www.cascadedesigns.com
Manufacturer of SealLine
water bags and products.

Cheaper Than Dirt

2524 NE Loop 820,
Fort Worth, TX 76106
Phone: 800-421-8047
Fax: 800-596-5655
www.CheaperThanDirt.com
Military surplus.

Chris Reeve Knives

11624 W. President Drive,
Suite B, Boise, ID 83713
Phone: 208-375-0367
Fax: 208-375-0368
www.chrisreeve.com
Manufacturer of custom/
production knives.

Christy Company (The)

905 Dickinson Street,
Fremont, Ohio, 43420
Phone: 419-332-8281
Fax: 419-332-6268
Manufacturer of the Christy
survival knife.

CMG Equipment

Recently acquired by Gerber

Legendary Blades
14200 SW 72nd Ave.,
Portland, OR 97224
www.cmgequipment.com
Manufacturer of Infinity
LED Task Light and Sonic light.

Coghlan's Ltd

121 Irene Street,
Winnipeg, Canada R3T 4C7
Phone: 204-284-9550
Fax: 204-475-4127
Manufacturer/distributor of
outdoor camping gear.

Cold Steel

3036-A Seaborg Avenue,
Ventura, CA 93003
Phone: 800-255-4716
www.coldsteel.com
Manufacturer of knives.

Columbia River Knife & Tool

9720 S.W. Hillman Court,
Suite 805,
Wilsonville, OR 97070
Phone: 503-685-5015
Fax: 503-682-9680
www.crkt.com
Manufacturer of knives.

Diamond Machining Technology, Inc.

85 Hayes Memorial Drive,
Marlborough, MA 01752
Phone: 508-481-5944
Fax: 508-485-3924
www.dmtsharp.com
Manufacturer of knife sharpeners.

EMS – Eastern Mountain Sports

Stores located around the U.S.
Phone: 888-463-6367

www.ems.com
Full line of camping equipment,
Nalgene bottles.

Essential Gear, Inc.
22 Cleveland Street
Greenfield, MA 01301
Phone: 413-722-8984
Fax: 413-772-8947
www.essentialgear.com
Distributor for Adventure
Lights such as the Guardian
mini strobe.

Exploration Products
P.O. Box 32090,
Bellingham, WA 98228
Phone: 800-448-7312
Fax: 360-676-4400
www.epcamps.com
Full line of survival kit
components, Mini Glass Vial for
repackaging Potable Aqua tablets,
Emergency Sunglasses, Esbit
Folding Pocket Stove, Gill Net,
Sawvivor, Lifeboat matches,
Nuwick-44 candle, Skyblazer
Wilderness XLT Flares, SpeedHook,
Thompson Snares, two-gallon
water bag.

Four Seasons Survival
1857 Park Forest Avenue,
State College, PA 16803
Phone: 814-234-0698
www.fourseasonssurvival.com
Manufacturer of SparkLite
Firestarter and Tinder-Quik
Fire Tabs.

Franklin Covey
Government Products Group
350 East Elliot Road,
Chandler, AR 85225-1103
Phone: 800-872-0232
Fax: 480-892-3791

www.gov.franklincovey.com
Manufacturer of various shoulder
bags and pouches.

Garmin International, Inc.
1200 East 151st Street,
Olathe, Kansas 66062
Phone: 913-397-8200
Fax: 913-397-8282
www.garmin.com
Manufacturer of GPS units.

Gerber Legendary Blades
14200 S.W. 72nd Avenue,
Portland, OR 97224
Phone: 800-950-6161
Fax: 503-684-7008
www.gerberblades.com
Manufacturer of knives and
multi-tools.

Henry Repeating Arms Company
110 8th Street,
Brooklyn, NY 11215
Phone: 718-499-5600
Fax: 718-768-8056
www.henryrepeating.com
Manufacturer of Henry U.S.
Survival Rifle.

Innovative Products, Inc.
50 N. Harrison Street,
York, PA 17403
Phone: 717-843-2745
Fax: 717-845-7900
Manufacturer of folding,
wood-burning Pocket Cooker.

Jensen Tools
7815 46th Street,
Phoenix, AZ 85044-5399
Phone: 800-426-1194
Fax: 800-366-9662
www.jensentools.com

Distributor of tools and Mighty Tuff parts boxes.

Ka-Bar Knives, Inc.
200 Homer Street,
Olean, NY 14760
Phone: 716-372-5952
Fax: 716-790-7188
www.kabar.com
Manufacturer of knives.

Katadyn North America, Inc.
9850 51st Avenue North,
Minneapolis, MN 55442
Phone: 800-755-6701
Fax: 763-746-3540
www.katadyn.com
Manufacturer of Micropur water-purification tablets and various filters such as the Hiker.

Kershaw Knives
25300 S.W. Parkway Avenue,
Wilsonville, OR 97070
Phone: 800-325-2891
www.kershawknives.com
Manufacturer of knives.

London Bridge Trading Company Ltd.
3509 Virginia Beach Blvd.,
Virginia Beach, VA 23452
Phone: 757-498-0207
Fax: 757-498-0059
www.londonbridgetrading.com
Manufacturer of nylon tactical gear.

Mag Instrument, Inc.
1635 South Sacrament Avenue,
P.O. Box 50600,
Ontario, CA 91761
Phone: 909-947-1006
Fax: 909-947-3116
www.maglite.com
Manufacturer of the Maglite flashlight.

McNett Corporation
1411 Meador Avenue,
Bellingham, WA 98229
Phone: 360-671-2227
Fax: 360-671-4521
www.mcnett.com
Manufacturer of Aquamir water treatment, Frontier Emergency Water Filtration System and SeamGrip products.

Mountain House
525 25th Avenue, SW,
Albany, OR 97321
Phone: 800-547-0244
Fax: 541-812-6601
www.mountainhouse.com
Manufacturer of freeze-dried food.

Mountaineers Books (The)
1001 SW Klickitat Way,
Suite 201,
Seattle, WA 98134
Phone: 800-553-4453
Fax: 800-568-7604
www.mountaineersbooks.org
Publisher of outdoor books.

MPI Outdoors
10 Industrial Drive,
Windham, NH 03087
Phone: 800-343-5827
Fax: 603-890-0477
www.mpioutdoors.com
Manufacturer of SPACE brand emergency blankets, Safe Signal mirror, Esbit Folding Pocket Stove and Emergency Strobe.

MSR – Mountain Safety Research
4000 1st Avenue S.,
Seattle, WA 98134
Phone: 800-531-9531
Fax: 800-583-7583
www.msrcorp.com
Manufacturer of various backpacking

and camping products such as water filters and purifiers, mini gas stoves, titanium cookware, pack towels, etc.

NALGENE Outdoor Products
Nalge Nunc International Corp.,
75 Panorama Creek Drive,
Rochester, NY 14625
Phone: 800-625-4327
www.nalgene-outdoor.com
Manufacturer of Nalgene bottles and products.

New Sun Productions
251 Upper North Road,
Highland, NY 12528
Phone: 845-691-7278
Fax: 845-691-4694
www.newsungear.com
Manufacturer of belt pouches and small packs.

North Face (The)
2013 Farallon Drive,
San Leandro, CA 94577
Phone: 800-447-2333
www.thenorthface.com
Manufacturer of adventure clothing and equipment.

Nuwick Incorporated
P.O. Box 7962,
Van Nuys, CA 91409
Phone: 818-980-3314
Fax: 818-980-2940
www.nuwick.com
Manufacturer of Nuwick-44 and Nuwick-120 candles.

Ontario Knife Company
P.O. Box 145,
Franklinville, NY 14737
Phone: 800-222-5233
Fax: 716-676-5535

www.ontarioknife.com
Manufacturer of Air Force Survival Knife and line of Randall Adventure Knives to include RTAC, TAC and RAT.

Outdoor Research
2203 1st Ave., South,
Seattle, WA 98134
Phone: 888-467-4327
Fax: 206-467-0374
www.orgear.com
Manufactures backpacking, camping gear, organizer bags and pouches, and soft brimmed packable hats.

Orion Safety Products
P.O. Box 1047,
Easton, MD 21601
Phone: 800-22-ORION
www.orionflares.com
Manufacturer of Skyblazer Flares, whistles, dye markers, etc.

Otter Products, LLC
Bldg. 1, Old-Town Square,
Suite 303,
Fort Collins, CO 80524
Phone: 888-695-8820
Fax: 888-695-8827
www.otterbox.com
Manufacturer of Otter Box waterproof cases.

Pelican Products, Inc.
23215 Early Avenue,
Torrance, CA 90505
Phone: 310-326-4700
Fax: 310-326-3311
www.pelican.com
Manufacturer of waterproof cases.

Platypus
www.platypushydration.com
Manufacturer of flexible hydration systems.

COMPONENT SUPPLIERS

Polar Equipment, Inc.

www.polarequipment.com
Manufacturer of Polar Pure
water disinfectant. Sells only
through retailers such as Campmor,
EMS, etc.

PrincetonTec Sport Lights

P.O. Box 8057,
Trenton, NJ 08650
Phone: 609-298-9331
Fax: 609-298-9601
www.princetontec.com
Manufacturer of sport lights such as
the Blast and Attitude flashlights.

Ranger Joe's International

325 Farr Road,
Suite A,
Columbus, GA 31907
Phone: 800-247-4541
Fax: 706-682-8840
www.rangerjoe.com
Survival components, Lifeboat
matches, military survival saw,
navigation, Nuwick-44 candles,
parachute cord, Pocket ChainSaw.

Raymond Thompson Co., Inc.

15815 2nd. PL. W.,
Lynnwood, WA 98037
Phone: 425-745-5477

Schrade Knives & Tools
(AKA: Imperial Schrade Corp.)

7 Schrade Court,
Ellenville, NY 12428
Phone: 845-647-7600
Fax: 845-210-8671
www.schradeknives.com
Manufacturer of knives
and tools.

Snow Peak, USA, Inc.

4754 Avery Lane,
Lake Oswego, OR 97035

Phone: 503-697-3330
Fax: 503-699-1396
www.snowpeak.com
Manufacturer of high-end camping
and cooking gear to include the
miniature titanium GigaPower
gas-canister stove.

SOG Specialty Knives
& Tools, Inc.

6521 212th Street Southwest,
Lynwood, WA 98036
Phone: 425-771-6230
Fax: 425-771-7689
www.sogknives.com
Manufacturer of specialty knives
including SOG Seal Revolver.

S.O.S. Food Lab, Inc.

9399 NW 13th Street,
Miami, FL 33172
Phone: 305-594-9933
Fax: 305-594-7667
www.sos-rations.com
Manufacturer of Emergency Food
Rations and water packets.

Spec.-Ops. Brand
Best Made Designs, LLC

1601 W. 15th Street,
Monahans, TX 79756
Phone: 915-943-4888
Fax: 915-943-5565
www.specopsbrand.com
Manufacturer of nylon
tactical gear, such as the
Better BDU Belt and BDU
Cargo Pocket Organizer.

Springfield Armory

420 West Main Street,
Geneseo, IL 61254
Phone: 800-680-6866
Fax: 309-944-3676
www.springfield-armory.com
Manufacturer of M6 Scout Survival
Rifle.

COMPONENT SUPPLIERS

Supreme Products

P.O. Box 550,
Sterling Heights, MI 48311
Phone: 248-588-1150
Fax: 248-588-3559
www.supremeprod.com
Manufacturer of Pocket Chain Saw
in a can.

Sun Company, Inc.

14025 West 66th Avenue,
Arvada, CO 80004-1049
Phone: 303-424-4651
Fax: 303-467-1104
www.suncompany.net
Manufacturer/importer
of compasses.

Survival Inc.

2633 Eastlake Avenue East,
Suite 103,
Seattle, WA 98102
Phone: 800-292-4707
Fax: 206-726-0130
www.ultimatesurvival.com
Manufacturer of BlastMatch Fire
Starter, Strike Force Fire Starter,
WetFire Tinder, StarFlash Signal
Mirror, JetStream Whistle.

Survival Sheath Systems

10117 Cougar Place,
Anderson Island, WA 98303
Phone: 253-884-9178
Fax: 253-884-6774
www.survivalsheaths.com
Custom manufacturer of knife
sheaths for survival purposes,
including a sheath with a
survival kit.

Survivor Industries, Inc.

4880 Adohr Lane,
Camarillo, CA 93012
Phone: 805-484-6977
Fax: 805-484-9906
www.survivorind.com

Manufacturer of Mainstay
Emergency Food Rations and
Emergency Drinking Water,
Cocoon pocket sleeping bag,
emergency thermal blanket
and various survival kits.

Suunto USA

2151 Las Palmas Drive,
Suite F,
Carlsbad, CA 92009
Phone: 800-543-9124
Fax: 760-931-9875
www.suuntousa.com
Manufacturer of Suunto compasses.

Swiss Army Brands, Inc.

65 Trap Falls Road,
Shelton, CT 06484
Phone: 800-442-2706
Fax: 203-926-1505
www.swissarmy.com
U.S. distributor of Victorinox
products.

Timberline Knives

(Now owned by GATCO – Great
American Tool Company, Inc.)
P.O. Box 600, Getzville, NY 14068
Phone: 716-877-2200
www.timberlineknives.com
Manufacturer of knives.

TOPS – Tactical OPS USA

P.O. Box 2544,
Idaho Falls, ID 83403
Phone: 208-542-0113
Fax: 208-552-2945
www.topsknives.com
Manufacturer of custom and
production knives.

Underwater Kinetics

13400 Danielson Street,
Poway, CA 92064
Phone: 858-513-9100

COMPONENT SUPPLIERS

www.uwkinetics.com
Manufacturer of lights and cases, such as 2 AAA Mini Pocket Light.

Victorinox AG
(For U.S. distributor see Swiss Army Brands, Inc.)
Schmiedgasse 57,
CH-6438 Ibach-Schwyz
Phone: +41 41 81 81 211
Fax: +41 41 81 81 511
www.victorinox.com
Manufacturer of knives.

Warren Cutlery Corporation
P.O. Box 289, Rhinebeck, NY 12572
Phone: 845-876-3444
Fax: 845-876-5664
www.warrencutlery.com
Manufacturer of cutlery to include replacement carving blades.

WPC Brands
1 Repel Road, P.O. Box 198,
Jackson, WI 53037
www.wpcbrands.com
Manufacturer of Potable Aqua, Repel and Atwater Carey products.

ZZ Manufacturing, Inc.
P.O. Box 1798,
Glendora, CA 91740
Phone: 800-594-9046
Fax: 626-852-2428
www.zzstove.com
Manufacturer of the Sierra wood-burning survival stove.

APPENDIX III

SURVIVAL TRAINING and READING

Be sure to check out any survival school before you attend to ensure the school offers the type of training you are seeking. Some schools offer wilderness survival skills while others specialize in desert, jungle, water or winter skills. Some schools offer only primitive skills while some offer only modern skills. Know what type of training you desire. Analyze the actual curriculum to verify it meets your specific needs. Are the courses taught in a classroom or out in the field, and what are you looking for? Ask for references from former students. Is the owner featured in the brochure an instructor or does he just stop by for philosophical support?

The following is a list of survival schools that have been around awhile. Listing these schools does not mean the author or the publisher endorse them or their services. Keep in mind that learning survival skills can be dangerous and you should make a selection based on that knowledge. If you participate, it will be at your own risk.

The following schools are listed in alphabetical order and not by level of expertise.

SURVIVAL TRAINING

Aboriginal Living Skills School
P.O. Box 3064, Prescott, AZ 86302
Phone: 520-636-8384
www.alssadventures.com
Offers both primitive and modern wilderness survival courses.

Boulder Outdoor Survival School (BOSS)
P.O. Box 1590, Boulder, CO 80306
Phone: 303-444-9779
Fax: 303-442-7425
www.boss-inc.com
Offers survival skills and field courses.

Hoods Woods
P.O. Box 3683,
Coeur D'Alene, ID 83814

Phone: 888-257-BUGS
www.survival.com
Although Ron Hood no longer offers wilderness survival programs, he does offer, in my opinion, the finest series of wilderness survival training videos available. Known as the Woodsmaster Video Series, each video covers a specific area of survival or wilderness skills.

Northwest School of Survival – ITP
2870 NE Hogan Road, E-461,
Gresham, OR 97030
Phone: 503-668-8264
Fax: 503-668-1226
www.nwsos.com
Offers many different survival

TRAINING & READING

courses to include wilderness survival.

Randall's Adventure & Training
60 Randall Road, Gallant, AL 35972
Phone: 256-570-0175
www.jungletraining.com
Offers jungle survival training. All training performed in Peru.

School of Self Reliance
P.O. Box 41834,
Eagle Rock, CA 90041
Phone: 323-255-9502
Fax: 323-402-1223
www.self-reliance.net
Offers courses on self-reliance.

Simply Survival
P.O. Box 882, Stevenson, WA 98648
Fax: 509-427-4155
www.simplysurvival.com
Offers various survival courses to include wilderness survival.

Tom Brown's Tracker School
P.O. Box 173, 92 Valley Station Road,
Asbury, NJ 08802
Phone: 908-479-4681
Fax: 908-479-6867
www.trackerschool.com
Offers survival and tracking courses with a philosophical approach.

Wilderness Learning Center
435 Sandy Knoll Road,
Chateaugay, NY 12920
Phone: 518-497-3179
www.weteachu.com
Offers 7-day basic and 10-day advanced wilderness survival and winter skills courses.

SURVIVAL READING

The following is a list of some of the books that cover various aspects of survival skills. Again, no recommendations are being made and these books are listed only because they either offer information on survival skills or skills that will help you survive, such as first aid, navigation, etc. They are listed in alphabetical order, not by subject matter.

Camp Life in the Woods and the Tricks of Trapping
By: W. Hamilton Gibson
Lyons Press, P.O. Box 480,
Guilford, CT 06437
ISBN: 1-58574-482-4 (pbk.)
First published in 1881, it is an illustrated guide on how to catch everything from tigers and bears to squirrels and mice, and offers general advice on camping and hiking in the woods. Includes many easy-to-follow examples for making snares.

Mountaineering First Aid
By: Jan D. Carline, Ph.D., Martha J. Lentz, R.N., Ph.D., & Steven C. Macdonald, M.P.H., Ph.D.
The Mountaineers, 1001 SW Klickitat Way, Suite 201
ISBN: 0-89886-478-X
A guide to wilderness first aid.

Mountainman Crafts & Skills
By: David Montgomery
The Lyons Press, P.O. Box 480,
Guilford, CT 06437
ISBN: 1-58574-066-7 (pbk.)
An illustrated guide to mountain-

man skills for wilderness living and survival.

Naked Into the Wilderness – Primitive Wilderness Living & Survival Skills

By: John & Geri McPherson
Prairie Wolf, P.O. Box 96, Randolph, KS 66554
ISBN: 0-9678777-7-6
A guide to primitive survival skills.

Outdoor Survival Skills

By: Larry Dean Olsen
Chicago Review Press, Inc., 814 North Franklin Street, Chicago, IL 60610
ISBN: 1-55652-323-8
A basic guide to outdoor survival skills.

Peterson Field Guides to Edible Wild Plants (available for various regions of the United States)

By: Lee Allen Peterson
Houghton Mifflin Company, Boston & New York
ISBN: Depends on the region you want.
Well-illustrated guide to edible plants.

SAS Essential Survival

By: Barry Davies, BEM
Lewis International, 2201 NW 102nd Place #1, Miami, FL 33172
ISBN: 1-930983-10-7
A practical guide to survival techniques for various situations.

SAS Survival Guide

By: John Wiseman
Harper Collins Publishers, P.O. Box, Glasgow G4 ONB
ISBN: 0-00-472302-3
Thorough pocket guide to survival.

Stalking the Healthful Herbs

By: Euell Gibbons
Alan C. Hood & Company, Inc., Chambersburg, Pennsylvania.
ISBN: 0-911469-06-0
A guide on the nutritional and medicinal properties of wild herbs and plants.

Stalking the Wild Asparagus

By: Euell Gibbons
Alan C. Hood & Company, Inc., Chambersburg, Pennsylvania.
ISBN: 0-911469-03-6
A guide to the recognition, gathering, preparation and use of natural health foods that grow wild.

Survival Psychology

By: John Leach
New York University Press, Washington Square, New York, NY 10003
ISBN: 0-8147-5090-7
Deals with understanding the psychological factors that affect those facing a survival situation.

Surviving Cold Weather

By: Gregory Davenport
Stackpole Books, 5067 Ritter Road, Mechanicsburg, PA 17055
ISBN: 0-8117-2635-5 (pbk.)
A basic guide to cold-weather survival.

The Complete Book of Outdoor Survival

By: J. Wayne Fears
Krause Publications, 700 E. State Street, Iola, WA 54990
ISBN: 0-87341-849-2
Provides information on basic survival skills for outdoor enthusiasts, to include various environments such as arctic, desert, water, swamp, mountain, etc.

TRAINING & READING

The Complete Wilderness Training Book
By: Hugh McManners
DK Publishing Inc., 95 Madison Avenue, New York, NY 10016
ISBN: 0-7894-3750-3
A guide to basic survival skills with many color photos.

The Essential Wilderness Navigator – 2nd Edition
By: David Seidman with Paul Cleveland
Ragged Mountain Press, P.O. Box 220, Camden, ME 04843
ISBN: 0-07-136110-3 (alk. paper)
A guide to how to find your way in the great outdoors with a map and compass.

The Outdoor Survival Handbook
By: Raymond Mears
St. Martin's Press, 175 Fifth Avenue, New York, NY 10010
ISBN: 0-312-09359-4
A guide to the resources and materials available in the wild and how to use them for food, shelter, warmth and navigation.

Tom Brown's Field Guide – Wilderness Survival
By: Tom Brown, Jr., with Brandt Morgan
Berkley Publishing Group, 375 Hudson Street, New York, NY 10014
ISBN: 0-425-10572-5
A guide to basic survival skills

United States Air Force Search and Rescue Survival Training
Reprint of the Department of the Air Force Field Manual – AF Regulation 64-4
Michael Friedman Publishing Group, Inc., 230 Fifth Avenue, New York, NY 10001
ISBN: 1-58663-722-3
Large hardback reprint with lots of survival information geared toward a downed-pilot situation.

US Army Survival Manual Reprint of Department of the Army Field Manual FM 21-76
Dorset Press
ISBN: 1-56619-022-3
Lots of survival information geared to military circumstances.

Using a Map and Compass
By: Don Geary
Stackpole Books, 5067 Ritter Road, Mechanicsburg, PA 17055
ISBN: 0-8117-2591-X (alk. paper)
A basic guide to map and compass.

Wilderness Survival
By: Gregory J. Davenport
Stackpole Books, 5067 Ritter Road, Mechanicsburg, PA 17055
ISBN: 0-8117-2985-0 (pbk.)
A basic guide to survival skills.

Wildwood Wisdom
By: Ellsworth Jaeger
Shelter Publications, Inc., P.O. Box 279, Bolinas, CA 94924
ISBN: 0-936070-12-9
Provides an illustrated look into how the skills and ingenuity of early wilderness men allowed them to survive in early America.

Winter Wise – Travel and Survival in Ice and Snow
By: Montague "Monty" Alford
Heritage House Publishing Company Ltd., Unit #108 – 17655 66 A Ave., Surrey, BC V3S 2A7
ISBN: 1-895811-95-3
A good guide to winter survival.